Dear
Mommy
Dear
Daddy,

Dear Mommy Dear Daddy,

by Marie Foss Hafen

Illustrated by Kay Mac Vicars
Typesetting and Editing Consulting by Elaine Terry

♡ Written from your young child's heart

ISBN 1-886990-00-X
Copyright No. TX4-709-223
092489168

For speaking engagements please call 1-435-634-0853

First Printing, Revised Book 1998
Second Printing, Revised Book 1999
Third Printing, Revised Book 2001
Printing by
Publishers Press
U.S.A.

Dear Families,

I wrote this common sense parenting book because of my sincere concern for many mothers and fathers who need basic (easy to understand) parenting information. Because of my personal concerns I searched for this particular kind of book. Since I could not find one, I began my own pursuit. As I read numerous parenting, divorce, abuse and related books I realized most were possibly too clinical and not easy to comprehend for many people. Many parents have little time to read and so they become discouraged and confused as the pressures of being a parent are in front of them daily. After a great deal of research and contemplation, I was struck by a thought, "What if the book was written as if by the baby and young child?" I realized this sweet and honest approach would be helpful in teaching common sense values. I immediately began to write down simple thoughts and feelings from the young child's perspective. This has been a heartfelt project with considerable thought and research, the seeking of expert opinions and our continual prayers.

Gratitude must be expressed to my many friends for their professional opinions and advice. Likewise, I consider the multiplicity of books I researched and the authors who wrote them to also be my friends. Deepest heartfelt appreciation goes to my dutiful typesetter and proof reader, Elaine Terry. Many friends acted as editing consultants and proof readers as they devoted personal sacrificing hours. As mothers and grandmothers we all agree that this is the book we wish we could have had as we reared our many children!

I must express my gratefulness to my husband Ralph R. Hafen. I respect his loyalty, patience and wise suggestions as I continued on this long journey of research and writing. Also, Ralph's five children and their families have been very supportive and thoughtful.

This book is intended to offer a good common sense foundation in understanding the needs of children, which can be enhanced with parenting classes and create an interest in other valuable parenting books. The hope is that less mistakes will be made as better parenting understanding is gained. My five children have been the joy of my life and they have not only been very supportive but have helped me filter areas from our past experiences together (some pleasing, some displeasing). We have learned a lot from one another. Being a young mother and not having family around to answer my questions was perplexing at times. This book is what I learned from neighbors and friends and parenting books, but there was so much basic information I wish I could have had. This book reflects the heart of many Grandmothers (like me) who want to pass their learned parenting knowledge along to the next generation.

Babies are born pure and innocent and completely dependent on their parents. (They are a gift from God.) Parents owe it to their babies to do all they can to provide for them and to attain values of honesty, integrity, virtue, morality and to develop skills and/or education to work for a living. An atmosphere should be created where children can feel safe and be able to trust those around them. If we choose to be parents, we owe it to the "little ones" to choose to be responsible!

It is my hope that parents will be willing to give their little children the very best, so the next generation can pass these good values along. (Each generation should try to make the next generation "better!") Children have a lot to say - are we willing to listen and to change? Children should be respected, loved and guided, (not abused or neglected in any way). They should be number one in your life. If you are doing your very best to teach values and change when you are wrong, I am very proud of you. Your children are the ones who will have a better future.

Thank you for Loving Children,

Marie Foss Hafen

Dedicated to all children.

Thank you to my children,
Shauna, Barry, Erick,
Brenda and Tonya
for all we have
learned together.

This book has been written for all parents.
If your little ones could talk from their hearts,
they would ask you to love and care for them.
Your job is to try to make the
next generation better and do your best.

Thank you for loving children!
Marie Foss Hafen

p.s. (Forgive your own parents for their shortcomings on rearing you - they did the best they could.)
The principles in this book apply to everyone from infancy to old age.

TABLE OF CONTENTS

I. MY BABY BEGINNINGS and Basic Mommy Pregnancy Information

This is only the "beginning" of this unique and useful parenting book...

Please keep reading so you can understand the feelings and needs of little children...

Read more...and see how little ones feel about moving, divorce and abuse (what do parents do when they are in a difficult situation?)

Keep going...you can learn "how" to keep the house clean & neat the easy way (see the good ideas and hints)...

AND...you can cook healthful foods, save money and learn about the importance of mealtime in the home...

Also...Look over Grandma's Treasured Hints
Many Grandma's have been passing these good hints down through the ages. It is helpful to listen to those who have already been there...

Dear Mommy, Dear Daddy,

All kinds of babies come to this world.

(The world says "thank you" when you accept responsibility by working, providing and caring for me!)

It is important to take parenting seriously. (Babies are little people - not toys.)

Always remember parenting is for your lifetime, (even as a grandparent).
I should be more important to you than your hobbies, your job, your friends or recreation. I need you.

I am perfect and pure when I come to you as a tiny new baby.

Dear Mommy, Dear Daddy,

Did you know God gave me to you to learn how to be a kind and responsible person? (This book will help you.)

There are all kinds of families.

Studies prove that children who live with two responsible and loving parents do much better when they go to school (and continuing through life).

A family consists of two Parents (Birth or adoption), Single Parent, Foster care, relatives, etc., but having both a Mother and a Father is the very best.

Families care for babies by providing food, warmth, clean surroundings, and lots of love. ♡

Pregnant Moms need to take care of themselves.

After reading the HINTS FOR THE HOME section in the back of this book (pages 125-141) we need to BE READY before the baby comes. The simple cooking & cleaning ideas are great!

See a doctor or clinic as soon as you are pregnant. Don't take drugs, smoke or use alcohol. (Protect both mom and baby). Please eat foods that are good for you. When you eat foods that are good for you, you are also helping your unborn baby to grow healthy. Take a multi-vitamin and Folic Acid each day (fresh orange juice, dark green leafy vegetables & beans).

Some moms get real sick when they get pregnant.

A little nausea is normal.
If you can't hold any food down tell the doctor or nurse.
(For most women the nausea may last 3 to 4 months)

Moms need to know how fast a baby develops.

Month 1	Brain, eyes, mouth, inner ears, arms and legs beginning to form.
Month 2	Face, elbows, knees, fingers and toes are forming. Bones are beginning to harden. Baby can move!
Month 3	Teeth, lips, genitals are forming. Baby can kick legs, make a fist, turn head and squint and frown!

My heart starts beating during the first month.
(Isn't that exciting?)

This is so wonderful!

Month 4	Hair, eyebrows, eyelashes, fingernails & toenails forming. Taste buds. 7 inches, 4 ounces!
Month 5	Hair on head, kicks & turns a lot. Can suck thumb. 10-12 inches, ½ to 1 pound
Month 6	Baby opens & shuts eyes. Hears sounds inside mom. 11-14 inches, 1¼-1½ pounds
Month 7	Weight doubled, red wrinkled skin. 14-17 inches, 2½-3 pounds
Month 8	Hears sounds, bones are hard. 4½-6 pounds
Month 9	Skin is smooth. Baby turns upside down, ready to be born. 20-22 inches, 6-8 pounds

My development is very important. It cannot be rushed.
(full term babies usually have fewer problems)

Most moms think pregnancy lasts a long time. (9 months)

I will be patient & understanding toward my wife when the baby comes. I will try to help her more around the house, and help with the baby. I want us to try to have a date or a break together once a week. My marriage is important to me, because my wife is special to me.

A date can be going for a walk, visiting the library, having an ice cream cone or soda or visiting a friend (etc.). Simply have a little time together for sharing and caring. A loving and considerate relationship is what all children deserve.

Pregnancy gives you time to prepare for my birth. You are going to be responsible for another life and it is a big commitment.

(This means you will be unselfish enough to be thoughtful and kind to each other and yet understand my many needs. Seek counseling if you feel you are arguing too much, are often angry and/or feeling sad most of the time).

♡ Through the years, please do everything you can to avoid divorce.

Most moms are nervous and excited when it is time for delivery.

*Many women are choosing to have their babies at home. If this is your choice, find a qualified midwife. They are usually very skilled and personally sensitive to your needs. **(Ask your clinic or the nurse or check the yellow pages of your phone book: "Midwives")*

Birth is a miracle. With the support of family, friends, and medical staff, you can have a good experience. (I am worth it!)

Dear Mommy, Dear Daddy,

I am born and I am
happy to be here!
Thank you for having me!
Please be patient and understanding: Feed me
properly, change my diaper often and always
support my head and back whenever you pick
me up. Be nice to each other. I need a happy
and caring home. Thank you.

II. My Many
Baby Needs

Since I am very tiny...
I have many needs.
I need you to understand how important my first five years are.

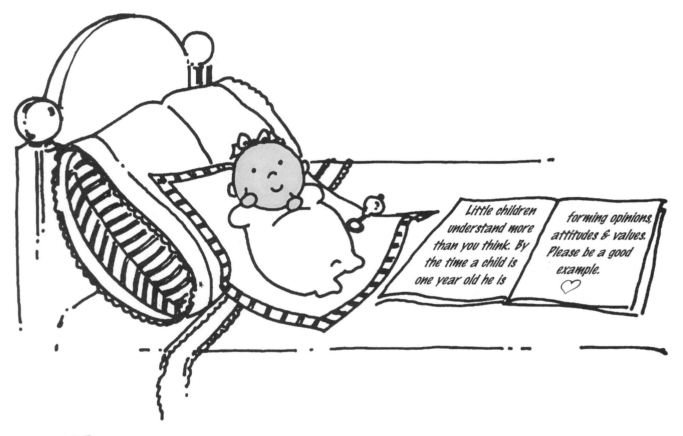

Little children understand more than you think. By the time a child is one year old he is forming opinions, attitudes & values. Please be a good example. ♡

♡ Please remember babies are angels who are pure and innocent. Babies "feel" everything we say or do. Act adult, discuss everything and seek for advice if you are not communicating.

♡ Talk to little ones the way you would like to be talked to. Realize it is not them always adjusting to your world, but you being mature enough to adapt to their world. Children deserve respect and consideration.

I need a clean bed and clean soft blankets.

Be careful when you buy old cribs. Some cribs have harmful lead paint or bars that are too wide. Never put me on a bean bag, down comforter, water bed or pillow to sleep - I could suffocate.

*Learn how to properly handle me. Always support my head and back whenever you gently pick me up and hold me.

*Please consult your doctor or clinic for the best position when I am put to bed. (It has been suggested that the best is my back or side).

I need to be changed and fed as soon as I wake up.

Thank you for taking good care of me.

*Ask the doctor or nurse the best way to burp me after every feeding.

Always gently wash baby's bottom with each diaper change.

Moms and Dads are both responsible for taking care of baby's needs. It's nice to help each other. Never ignore your baby's soggy diaper and cries for food. (Remember to wash your hands with soap and water after every diaper change).

*Some men need to learn how to be a "Daddy." Good Dads are very important in a child's life.

13

I need you to be gentle with me.

I am very fragile...if you get too upset when I am crying, and hit or shake me, OR hold me down or push me down (which can stop my breathing),

I could be badly injured or even die! I am too tiny to know the difference between 'bad' and 'good'. If I cry too much, it does not mean I am being bad; it just means I need you.

➔ When parents become tired or sick, they can become "frustrated." Frustration can lead to anger. If you feel extremely angry, go into the next room, go outside, or call a friend so you can calm down. Tell yourself, "...this is only a baby. I am the adult. I will never allow myself to hurt my baby!"

*Read pages 119 & 120

I Need to be Breast Fed if Possible.

1. Doctors agree mother's milk is best for the baby and most easily digested.

2. New mothers can get discouraged easily with breast feeding.

3. Call Le Leche League or an experienced nursing mother (call Health Department or call the Hospital and ask for a maternity floor nurse).

4. Don't be shy about telling someone your breast feeding frustrations (you are not alone!)

5. It takes about 2 - 4 weeks for you and baby to adjust.

6. It is recommended a baby should be breast fed at least one year. (Please continue to eat nutritious foods and drink plenty of water, juices and healthful liquids).

7. Remember, everything you eat or drink goes to your milk. Do not use alcohol, drugs or smoke when you are nursing. (If you require prescription drugs for an illness, tell the doctor you are nursing.)

14

I need special foods.

♡ Please keep my bottles clean. I should have a clean bottle for every feeding. When a bottle is left in my mouth (while I sleep) even good juice or formula can cause tooth decay. I should only have good things in my bottle to drink...formula, pure diluted (watered down) juices or water.

NEVER put soda pop, diet drinks, or mixed sugary punch in my bottle, especially NO beer or any liquor...they're not good for me.

*Never be shy about asking your doctor or nurse questions.

I need good food my First Year.

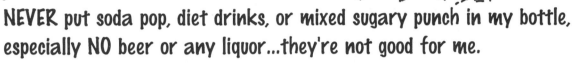

♡ Consult your doctor or clinic first.

Birth - 4 months	Breast milk or fortified formula (Breast milk is best for your baby.)
4 - 5 months	Baby rice cereal which has been mixed with baby formula (consistency of strained baby food)
5 - 7 months	Strained or pureed vegetables, fruits, watered down apple juice or unsweetened juice. (3 oz. a day)
7 - 8 months	Continue with the above foods but, add cottage cheese with pureed fruits, yogurt, strained meat, chicken, egg yolks (no whites until 1 year old)
8 - 9 months	Mashed fruits and vegetables, mild cheese, finger foods, tiny pieces of cooked vegetables, soft fruit. Offer juice in a cup.
10 - 12 months	Food from family table, cut up in tiny pieces (make sure it's chewable)
1 year	May be weaned from breast or bottle. Can drink other things.

* These foods are suggestions only.

* If I show allergies to any foods or drinks, tell the doctor.

* Don't feed honey to baby during first year.

* Always wash your hands with soap and water before preparing any food.

* Never force me to eat. Sometimes I will eat more, sometimes I will eat less. Simply feed me often.

* Pour a small amount of food in a seperate dish. Do not put the used spoon in the baby food jar. The bacteria can ruin the remaining food.

I need you to be very careful when you are warming my food.

The microwave will make some things very hot in certain spots. Be sure and stir and taste so my mouth won't get burned.

Hint: If food is too hot, put an ice cube in it and stir. Then remove the ice cube.

I need my face and hands washed if any food gets on me. I'm too tiny to do it.

A warm soft wash cloth is nice, or damp wipes work well when we travel.

*If a clean bib or small towel is placed on a child before eating or drinking, it will lessen possible stains on clothes. Replacing stained clothes can become an unnecessary expense.

*Also, most unstained baby clothes can be recycled for other babies.

 Thank you

16

I need you to let me move and wiggle.

I get bored sitting in my carrier all day.

Big blankets are fun to explore, but please don't leave me alone.

♡ Please don't leave me in a crib or bed too long.
I need a change of scenery,
but I especially need your love and attention.
I need a variety of bright safe toys. Please wash them every day. Thank you.

I need soft sounds.

When the television, radio, or anything is too loud, it is hard on my sensitive little body and mind.
Thank you for being considerate of me.

I need you to protect me.

<u>Please</u> pick up little stuff off the floor
that may get in my mouth and choke me.
<u>Please</u> cover the electric outlets
with plastic covers.
<u>Please</u> put all cleaning products and
poisons way up high where I can
NEVER reach them.
<u>Please</u> tie all cords up so I won't get
caught in the cord and possibly
get choked or strangled.
Do not allow me to play with plastic bags;
if I put it over my head I could stop breathing;
if I bite off a piece of plastic bag (or a
balloon) I could badly choke and/or strangle.

(Please never have a gun or other harmful things around me!)

Watch for all hanging
cords (especially irons).

I need you to protect me from pets.

When I am tiny I can't get away from animals.
They might hurt me "accidentally".
PLEASE don't EVER leave me
alone with a pet.

* House pets should be bathed and washed
often. Watch pets for any signs of illness,
which includes any signs of diarrhea or
vomiting. Scrub floors and carpet well to
remove all mess and possible worms or disease.
(This can be very harmful to the family.)

*Take any sick pet to the
Veterinarian immediately.

I need you to put labels on everything...

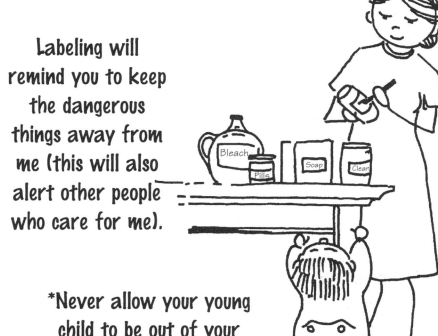

Labeling will remind you to keep the dangerous things away from me (this will also alert other people who care for me).

*Never allow your young child to be out of your sight too long.

Put these things up high and/or lock them up:

- All poisons
- Pill bottles
- Cleaning products
- Unusual food or liquids

Remember: All medicines can be dangerous and harmful.

I need you to be careful about buckets, toilets, or anything that holds water.

Young children can fall head first into toilets or buckets and drown quickly (this really can happen). NEVER leave a young child in the bathroom, even for a minute...

Keep bathroom door closed.

I need you to be patient while you teach me about things in the house that are special or fragile.

1. **Stop me gently.** (Please don't slap, yank or scream at me)
2. **Talk about the object.**
3. **Let me touch gently with one finger.**
4. **Move me to another area to play with something safe.**

*Put dangerous or valuable things up high or in a safe place

♡ Thank you for caring.

I need you to get into the habit of looking into my eyes and face when you talk to me.

When you smile, this makes me feel like I am someone special, and I want you to know you are special to me too. Please smile at me often. When Mom leaves and Dad is in charge, sometimes Dads can become very frustrated when the baby cries—read pages 14, 119 and 120 again. Sometimes Daddy needs to ask a lot of questions so he can be an effective parent.

I like it when you coo and babble along with me.

I need you to hold me and rock me often.

I like it when you hum & sing to me.

Sometimes I get fussy because I just want to be close to you. (I love you so much!)

Please don't get mad or upset when I cry or fuss. You are my Mommy and Daddy — I need you.

I need a sponge bath or a tub bath everyday.

It is nice to have the house or room warm while I am being bathed.

Even though I can't play outside I still need my baths. Don't ever leave me alone in the water (even for a second). I can be slippery in water, so handle me carefully. (Please use no-tear shampoo and baby soap.)

Never put me in water that is too <u>hot</u>! (or too <u>cold</u>)
(Put your elbow in the water to test it.)
Do not scrub me too hard. Wash me gently and securely, then wrap a towel around me to keep me warm. Dry me carefully. Dress me immediately so I won't become cold.

I need my diaper to be checked often.

Nothing feels better than a washed bottom and a dry diaper. It will also prevent diaper rash, pain and frustration.
(Babies need to be washed and handled "*gently*")

Hint: if you use cloth diapers, always rinse soiled diapers in the toilet and remove as much mess as possible before laundering. If diapers are very stained, soak them in a large container with a mild bleach solution, then launder as usual.
* Do laundry daily if possible.

I need you to understand that I am affected by your moods.

I don't expect you to be in a good mood all the time but when you're in a rotten mood, don't be mean or bad tempered with me...

Dear Mommy, Dear Daddy, I need you to understand that if you're upset with each other it's not fair to ignore me or take it out on me!

Babies can feel tension, hostile looks, and anger. Mature parents will resolve their conflicts quickly and still be loving toward the child. <u>Please</u> act like a mature parent.

*Remember, I feel what you feel. Your anger toward one another is hard on me.

I need you to take good care of yourself and take short breaks and have a little fun once in a while.

Remember, the younger I am, the harder it is for me to be away from you...
have short breaks from me so I don't feel scared.
As I get older I will feel safer when you leave.

WARNING! NEVER LEAVE ME HOME ALONE!

Do not leave me with someone too young or someone who has a disability that can
interfere with my care. Also Electronic Monitors are not baby-sitters.
(Leaving the monitor with a neighbor and leaving the baby alone is considered
child neglect because an accident can still happen)

I need you to be prepared when you leave me with someone.

Please remember

- Diaper Bag (or something)

- Bottle, formula, baby food, etc.

- Pacifier if needed

- Diapers and Wipes

- Ointment for diaper rash

- Baby Sunscreen

- Extra change of clothes

- Blankey (my blanket)

- Toy (my favorite one)

*Special instructions and/or medications, etc.

*Always check the weather: If it is cool or cold put socks or booties on my little feet. Place me in a large cozy blanket, or a sweater and cap or a bunting. Please keep me warm. Keep my feet warm. Keep my head warm. BUT, if it is hot don't bundle me too much. Use good sense.

*When it's windy, keep my ears covered (a little cap or something).

Thank you for being considerate of our caretakers.

I need you to be very careful when you leave me with someone.

I am still very fragile and sensitive. Maybe Grandma or a trusted friend could watch me once in a while for a short time. NEVER leave me with someone you don't know well.

♡ Please don't take advantage of caretakers or family, because staying away too long is not fair to them or me.

I need you to leave information for people who take care of me.

*Do not assume that care takers always know what to do, or what my routine is. Going over the Babysitter Chart helps all of us.

DEAR BABYSITTER or CARETAKERS

1. MY NAME IS _____ .
2. Mom/Dad will be home around _____ and it is OK for you to eat _____
   Thank you for helping me to feel safe while my Mom/Dad are out for awhile.
3. You can reach my Mom/Dad at _____ .
4. The neighbors (or friends) name is _____
   _____ and their number is _____
5. I usually go to bed at _____ and take my _____ with me.
6. The foods (or bottle) I can have are _____

   BUT I am allergic to _____ .
7. My favorite book(s) are: _____

8. My favorite cassette, TV show or video is _____

9. Other things I like to do are _____

I can show you where the toys are. Please help me to pick them up so things can look nice when Mommy/Daddy come home.
If I cry too much because I am a little bit afraid, please be patient with me. Sometimes it is hard for me to have them go (but I am glad they can have some fun)...
If I am taking medicine, please see special instructions from Mommy/Daddy.
Thank you.

I need you to take me to the doctor or clinic for my health check ups and immunizations (shots). Keep a simple record when I get sick (to show the Dr.)

Call your doctor or check with the County Health Department for services. (Look in the phone directory) ♡ This is very important.

I need you to keep a simple record when I get sick (to show the doctor).

Doctors are very busy. This will help them. When you take me to a doctor, clinic or nurse, be prepared to talk to them. They won't know unless you tell them. This is your time, you should ask questions about your baby.

ASK the doctor or nurse:

· When do I bring my baby in again? · Will this shot make my baby sick? · If so, what do I do for a fever, etc.? · Why is aspirin NOT good for my baby? · What do I do about diarrhea? · Explain why daily water and fluids are important for my baby. · What if my baby does not want to take his bottle, nurse or eat? · How do I give my baby medicine (show me how it is done)? · Explain to me why I should never give my baby ANY medicine without talking to you first, etc. · Encourage me to observe other babies the same age so I can see normal progress (smiling, watching objects, rolling over, sitting up, etc.) · Does the hospital or clinic have parenting classes?

♡ Remember: NEVER be embarrassed to ask any question.
No parent has all of the answers... Keep asking until you are satisfied and comfortable...
Find a way to attend parenting or Baby Your Baby classes.
Everyone learns from each other and it is "fun"!

I need you to understand that I may be fussy after my immunizations or checkups.

Ask the doctor what medicine will help me. Please arrange to stay close to me on these days. I need you.
♡ Thank you.

IMMUNIZATION SCHEDULE

Write down in the ♡ areas the date when you get my shots

Child's Name:

County Health Departments are in every city to help us. (Know which County you live in and call information - 411)

	DTP	Polio	Measles, Mumps, Rubella	HIB	Tetanius - Diphtheria	♡ HEP B
Birth						♡
1 Month	♡					♡
2 Months	♡	♡		♡		
4 Months	♡		♡			
6 Months	♡		♡			
15 Months	♡			♡		
4 - 6 Years						
14 - 16 Years						

♡ It is very important to keep this information for many years for:
- Kindergarten, Jr. High, College
- Military Service/Travel

- Serious illness or injury (Doctors & hospitals will always need this information)

Check with your Health Dept. or Dr. for changes in necessary immunizations.

Do not lose this information ever!

*Reminder — Remember to read all medicine bottles carefully and follow directions exactly as written. If you are confused or unsure, call your doctor's office.

I need you to <u>never</u> leave me in a car unattended.

Remember, cars can become very HOT like an oven or very COLD like a freezer. Use caution and <u>Never Leave Me Alone.</u>

It is very dangerous to leave a child (or a pet) alone in a car for any amount of time. <u>Please don't do this.</u>
♡ Thank You.

I need you to be PATIENT and UNDERSTANDING about my many needs and moods.

Your patience and kindness makes me feel secure and safe and happy.

I need a lot of rest when I am a baby or a young child. Many things make me very tired: after I eat, after you talk or play with me, going to the Doctor or Clinic, company coming to our home, any kind of shopping or any activity. (Please make sure I am fed and my diaper is changed before my naps).

♡ Thank you for being considerate of me... Make sure I have safe toys (nothing that can break or that has small parts).

I need you to remember my baby days.

The first year offers many challenges, and can test your patience. This is also a very special time because babies are cuddly and sweet. Take one day at a time and do your best. Babies grow so fast, try to write down, take pictures or video some memories. These memories will be priceless some day.

III. MY ⭐ WISHES

The following chapters are showing how I am getting bigger. As I begin to walk and explore I may not want to "cuddle" as much. Thank you for teaching me and helping me...

I wish you would teach me about the good things in this world.

Flowers
Moon
Stars
Sun
Clouds
Rain
Trees
Wind
Snow
Animals
Birds

People...All Kinds

There is so much beauty around us.
♡ Thank you for helping me to be aware of our world.

I wish you would keep a box (or something) for my special things.
(pictures, report cards, etc.)
I like to look at our family pictures.

Someday I will want to know everything about myself so I can share it with my children. My things will be more valuable to me than any expensive toy.

I wish you would teach me good manners.

Teach me to say...

~PLEASE~

~THANK YOU~

~YOU'RE WELCOME~

~EXCUSE ME~

~I'M SORRY~

You are my best example.
If you are kind and courteous and
use these words, I will do the same.

♡ Thank you

I wish our TV and phone were broken sometimes.

I have waited for you all day and I need your attention after dinner.

(This is my favorite time with you)

Love means paying attention to me and not ignoring me. I need to feel welcome and safe, and to feel free to cuddle and chat with you. I feel isolated and lonely when you are too busy for me.

I look forward to our play time, pick up toys time, reading time, bath time, tuck in bed time, and you tell me that you love me.

I wish you didn't get so mad sometimes about messes.

When we visit friends, teach me to pick up the toys before we leave.

♡ Thank you for teaching me to keep our home picked up and in order.

I don't know what "mess" means. I just need to "learn" how to pick up my things.

(I don't criticize when you make messes: kitchen, laundry, bathroom, etc.)

I guess we need to learn to understand each other.

Hint: Before I go to bed at night maybe we could play "pick up toys". I could use a bucket, little wagon or something that will hold the toys.

I wish you would be careful about what I watch on TV.

I don't want the TV to be my babysitter. Please make sure I don't watch scary violent stuff! (even some cartoons aren't good) I don't **KNOW** it's all _pretend_.

I wish you would choose the very best TV, videos, and children's programs for me.

It's nice when we choose TV shows together.

♡ Thank you for caring about what goes into my mind.

I wish I didn't always get so hungry because I'm not big enough to fix food.

It's hard for me to wait sometimes while you think of something to cook... I get so hungry! I feel good when meals are planned ahead and prepared on time. I like to eat together and be happy.

I wish you could keep a list of the food we need. This will help us when we do our shopping.

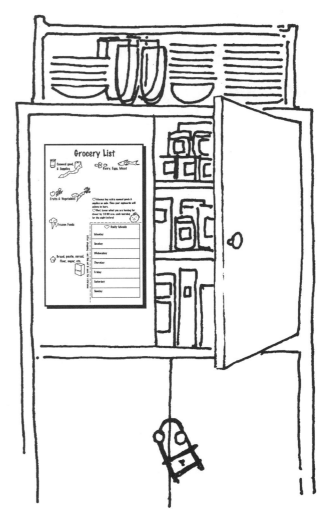

♡ Thank you for planning ahead...

I wish I was big enough to do the laundry...

...because it upsets me when you are mad and can't find anything to wear. I wish we could do laundry on a special day (each week), so we can be clean and happy.

p.s. Do you think we could lay our clothes out at night so we aren't so rushed in the mornings?

Many families wash, dry and fold clothes every day.
*The dirty clothes won't pile up and become such a work burden.

I wish mornings weren't so rushed.

I know you have to work and take me to daycare, but does everyone have to be so grouchy sometimes?

(Grouchy days make my tummy hurt and it's not good for me to eat too fast)

I have little legs and can't walk as fast as you. Please walk slower and stop once in awhile

I wish you would never forget to kiss or hug me (or both) when you drop me off at daycare or anywhere.

When I am little I like you to show me that you care.

(When I get bigger I still need to know that you care.)

If you have days you are upset with me, please NEVER THREATEN ME that you are <u>not</u> going to return to pick me up; OR you are going to leave me somewhere and drive away, etc.
<u>This is emotional abuse!</u>

*A child needs to hear many times a day how much they are loved and that you will always be there for them (over and over again). Parents are a child's "Hero". Always be a loving (and strong) hero! Your child will thank you some day...

♡ Thank you.

39

Dear Mommy, Dear Daddy,
I wish you would choose very carefully who will watch me while you are at work.

There are many
good day care places
and people, **BUT** sometimes
things are not what you think.
Always ask questions and check in or stop by often.

(Remember, we have choices - we can find someone who is exactly right for us.)

You are my only protection!

- Be Bold > Ask your company if they plan to provide on-site day care!
- Young children (especially babies) need their mother many times during a day.
  It is recommended that nursing mothers nurse their baby for at least a year.
- The day care should provide a child "sick care" area and an on site nurse.
- Studies have proven there are fewer absentees, less employee stress, highter morale,
  and increased production which provides a win/win for everyone!
- Companies with on-site day care wish they would have provided this service years ago.

I wish you would not swear and use bad words.

People who use good language appear more mature, and will receive more respect from others.

I wish you wouldn't argue around me.

Please settle your differences away from me. It scares me. (even when I'm a baby I can feel your anger) Everyone has differences— you just need to work them out peacefully.

Be mature enough to "listen" to one another. Take turns talking (AND listening). It is OK for one another to have different opinions – simply respect the other opinion, and observe your personal belief. Arguing may lead to unkind remarks that can damage your relationship. Share and Care...

*If you still feel angry, please get help.
*If one person dominates and doesn't listen to the other, please get help.

I wish you would get help if you're angry too much.

Strong people get help. When you get help, it helps me. ♡Thank you.

Families Should Be Forever

Happy Marriage:
1. Laugh together - enjoy one another's humor.
2. Enjoy playing together (games, athletic events, recreation).
3. Share everything - no competition or ownership. (Unselfish & Thoughtful)
4. Enjoy seeing one another each day - love to "share" the day's events.
5. Say something kind to each other every day - think & give compliments more than criticism.
6. Never criticizes partner to others - only says nice things. (Mature enough to talk to spouse instead)
7. Forgive & forget easily and make love more than argue. (Considerate of one another)
8. Show patience & respect even when the other may behave immaturely.
9. Enjoy quiet moments together and allow one another time to read or relax.
10. Mature adults take the time to express honest feelings and to listen to one another. (This is not to prove who is right or wrong, this is to improve your attitudes and treatment of one another).

As parents, the best gift you can give your child is to show love toward one another.

(It teaches them to know how to be loving.) This will help children to feel safe and happy.

For many couples, most anger and frustration comes from:

(1) Financial Stresses (spending without consulting one another, overuse of credit cards, not taking care of what you have and having to purchase again);

(2) Selfishness and greed (wanting everything your way and being too demanding or abusive and not being considerate of one another's sexual feelings);

(3) Unfaithfulness (flirting at work, having an affair, not coming home, not being truthful, etc.);

(4) Alcohol, drugs, gambling, etc. (addictions, eating disorders, pornography, etc.);

(5) Religious differences or no religion and a lost sense of values;

(6) Parenting differences (if you disagree on how to parent (bring up) your children, you will confuse your children and they may act out by rebelling and showing disrespect).

(7) Talk disrespectfully with sarcastic remarks, making accusations and assumptions, and saying mean or demeaning remarks - using profanity.

LEARN TO BE UNSELFISH; LEARN TO LET GO OF BAD HABITS; LEARN TO BE UNITED; LEARN TO BE GOOD PARENTS

I wish you didn't have to go to work so we could play and be together all day.

I am going to rearrange my work schedule (and my job duties), so I can spend more time with my family.

If you don't "have" to work full time, maybe one of you could work part time. If you don't "need" to work - then don't! I need you.

I understand that sometimes parents don't have a choice, so I am proud of you because you are trying to do what is best.

I can see that you work very hard for us.

Please come home after work. Tell your friends you cannot go places with them all the time, because your family needs you.

♡Thank you.

I wish our home, garage and yard were always safe...

- Do we have a camping ice chest? Is it put away so it can't be opened by a child who might crawl inside? Children can smother or suffocate in any closed appliance or chest (including a file cabinet!)
- Do we have an empty refrigerator or freezer. Is the door facing a wall so no one can open the door & crawl inside?
- Are sharp and heavy tools in a safe place?
- Are propane (or any gas tank) fixed so a child cannot turn the knobs? Are lawn mowers or anything mechanical stored safely?
- Are all paints & paint thinner stored in a safe area away from the house & garage?
- Are guns, knives or any weapon locked away?
- Do not put poisons, insecticides, etc. in pop bottles or other unmarked containers.
- Are ladders, ropes & wire safely stored?
- Is heavy furniture secured in case a child climbs onto it? (Many children climb at an early age.)
  Caution: Furniture may fall over on top of a child.

Keeping children safe is an important part of being a parent.

I wish you would look around our home and garage and yard.

hammer · heavy electrical tools · STORE & LABEL · rope · razors · BE SAFE · poisons · ladder · shovel · saw · paint · torches · wire · gas · rake · refrigerator · ice chest · nails · lawn mower

43

I wish I could remember your happy smile and sense of humor.

Peace on Earth begins with happy families.

I watch you a lot. I can feel when you're happy or sad or worried.
It makes me smile when you try to make things seem better.

I wish you would tell me "I LOVE YOU" everyday.

As long as I live I will **NEVER** get tired of hearing these words.

I need to hear that— thank you!

I LOVE YOU!

Please don't gossip about our friends and family.
I want to learn to be a forgiving and understanding person.
♡ Thank you for being a good example and talking nice about everyone.

I wish you could work at home.
(when I am small, I need you)

Hundreds of companies are looking for people to work-at-home.
Your library has many special books on ways to use your skills in your home.
Please Ask Now!
♡ **When you have to work outside the home,**
thank you for finding good people to take care of me.

45

I wish we would remember to "plan" (plan for fun too) so we will enjoy our home when we are together every day.

Cleaning the house and watching young children all day can be challenging.
Organizing "anything" makes the day go better. "You can do it!"
♡ For House Hints see pages 126-132 (Remember BDB...)

I wish you understood the importance of getting up when I'm up in the morning.

I need you every morning to take care of me.

(I am little) You can take a cat nap later.

Little children can GET INTO THINGS, and eat food that may not be good.

(This is when accidents can happen...) You may want to sleep in,

but it is better to take a nap in the afternoon when I nap.

I need to be fed and dressed every morning.

("Getting up" is what parents do.)

I wish you would remember my daily naps or quiet time.

It's nice when you read to me sometimes or play soft music on a cassette or radio.

Children feel better after a nap.
♡

It's best to have a nap right after lunch. Children get tired after a busy morning.
(It is important for growing bodies to have rest)

I wish I could tell you how happy I am that I was created to be your child.

I need a good self esteem: Please tell me your positive thoughts out loud. Please keep your negative thoughts to yourself. We will learn a lot from each other.

*I know I don't always do everything you want - but when I'm right, tell me. Reward me with a hug, smile, praise, thanks and your attention. Thank you. ♡

I wish you would be understanding while I learn to use the toilet.

Do not pressure, shame, hurt or tell me I am bad.
Gently encourage and praise me.
Most children learn with
patience and kindness.

(Most children are toilet trained
between 2 and 4 years old.)

♡ Please teach me to wash my hands often.

I wish you would be patient with my pacifier, thumb, or blankey.

I won't be needing these
things forever...
Right now they make
me feel safe,
so please don't shame me
when I need them.

It has been said: "Never criticize a child or scold
him for needing a "comfort thing".
(Being a little person and needing
a small comfort is OK).
*Normal scolding usually occurs when a child
may do something that may hurt himself,
hurt others, or damage
or break something.

49

I wish you could understand that my play is my work.

So much of what I know about this world is what I learn from my playtime. I love my toys and I like to touch and taste things. If something is dangerous for me, please put it where I can NEVER touch it!

I wish you wouldn't say "NO" and "DON'T" so much. Please show me what I CAN do and say "YES" more often.

I wish that when you make a promise you would always keep it.

If you keep your promises it will help me keep my promises as I get bigger.

I wish my Dad (or Grandpa or Uncle, etc.) would play and laugh with me more!

Studies have shown little children need a fun and playful relationship with their Daddy's *(or other loving Dad figure)* "Horseplay."

Crawling on the floor and hiding *(peek-a-boo)*, marching and clapping your hands, making fun out of "doing chores" *(picking up toys, putting clothes away, etc.)*, dancing to music, coloring together, playing dolls and/or cars, feeding time (in a fun way), happy dressing time, bath time with safe toys...

...holding a little one carefully up in the air, crawling after a little one, making funny faces and sounds, little "tickles" *(do not tickle too much)*, rolling a ball across the floor, and other safe and fun activities.

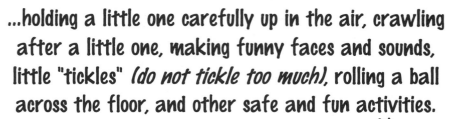

Acting like an animal can be fun. *(Don't be too scary. You can tell when a child is becoming frightened. If this happens tell them you are sorry and stop. Don't tease a child and call him hurtful names if something is scary or upsetting. Tell him you understand and you will be more careful).*

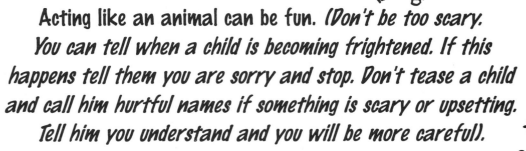

* When you play and laugh with children, they love it!

* Remember to not be bossy, "be fun and positive".

* When children show signs of becoming tired or cry, this is a clue they have had enough. Pick them up and hold them and talk gently about how much "fun" you have had with them. Don't get upset and say you won't play with them anymore. Be patient and understand because "you are the parent". (Tell them they can play again tomorrow).

* Dads who "make time" for their children are building a sweet relationship that can last forever.

* If there has been a separation or divorce, Dads should continue to be very involved with their children. If the Dad was abusive then special counseling and arrangements need to be considered. Never make a child feel he has to "choose"!

I wish you would remember I am curious and can wander away quickly anywhere.

(Stay close to me!)

Parks
Camping

Pools
Lakes
Beaches

Zoos
Fairs

Circus
Movies

Malls
Stores
Family Gatherings
Amusement Parks
Neighborhood

Please don't EVER let me go in a public restroom alone when we go to different places. Teach me to go to a <u>woman</u> if I ever get lost.
(A better chance to get SAFE help.)

Please be understanding and considerate of me when we go places. I get tired very quickly and need rest (& food).

♡ Safety devices are very important for children.

I wish you would have an I.D. for me.
(when we are in public places)

This card can be hung around my neck (under my clothes), or put in my pocket, etc. in case there is a problem or an emergency.

My Name
My Parents:

Home Phone #:

Mom's Work Phone #:

Dad's Work Phone #:

Neighbor, Friend or Relative #:

Medication &/or Allergies:

I wish you would teach me what you believe about God.

Who made this beautiful world?

Did God make you and me? Where is God?

People who have faith that life is a gift and something very good, seem to grow up to be positive adults with a purpose in life.

Some of the ways to learn about God and feel more spiritual are:

1. Learn to pray to Him.
2. Confess sins and get help to overcome bad habits.
3. Read scriptures and learn about making good choices in life.
4. Attend church, listen and look deep inside our personal selves.
5. Find ways to reach out and to help others – overcome being self centered.
6. Balance your life – work & play.
7. Know yourself – Love yourself.
8. Associate with people who believe in God.

I wish our home was our favorite place to be.

The greatest gift you can give a child is a loving home.

Being kind and considerate takes a lot of practice.

We manage our bills carefully.

We are kind to each other.

We talk nice in our home.

We share the housework without complaining.

When we get upset & yell – we give a "make-up hug"

Kind
Caring
Thoughtful
Mature
Unselfish

I wish you would teach me to show respect toward God and goodness.

- Help me to eat good food, exercise and get plenty of rest (and not let anyone do bad things to me.)

- Show me how to take care of our home, our belongings, and our car. Teach me how to plant flowers.

- Teach me not to litter. Teach me about our environment and recycling.

- Teach me to share with my friends and family. Teach me to be kind to animals and not hurt them.

- Teach me to have good manners and help me give service to others.

Take care of our home.

Show appreciation and gratitude.

Take care of the earth.

Take care of my body.

Be kind to others.

54

IV.
MY
LIKES

Children LOVE to do things with you.
Some of the ideas in this section
may be new to you.
GO AHEAD and do them anyway
(you will soon become comfortable with it).
Your child will love you for it!
Have Fun!

I like warm baths every night.

Bubble baths are fun once in a while.
I sleep better when I bathe at night.

NEVER put me in water that is too <u>HOT</u> or too <u>COLD</u> -
(put your elbow in the water to test it)
* Never leave young children alone in the bathtub.
*Too many bubble baths may cause skin irritations and vaginal infections.

I like ice cream and treats.

It's nice to have a treat
once in a while.
I don't need treats every day
but special occasions are fun.
*Treats can also be used as
"rewards" when I help you
around the house...

I like Hanukkah, Christmas and Easter and Halloween
and Thanksgiving and Valentines and Cinco de Mayo
and July 4th and ......

*I know it is extra
work and planning,
but we are worth it!

Celebrating holidays builds family traditions.
Family traditions build stronger families.

I like birthdays!

It doesn't take a lot of money to remember birthdays. Having a cake will make me feel special.

Every wonder how many children to invite? Hint: Do it by age.

1 yr. old — 1 friend
2 yr. old — 2 friends
3 yr. old — 3 friends, etc.

I like to be thoughtful.

Let's not forget other people's birthdays.

I am learning to think of others.

Remembering birthdays and special occasions makes everyone feel good. ♡ Our chart helps us to remember Birthdays.

I like it when we try to sing.

Don't worry if your voice isn't
perfect — I like it.
Thank you for buying
children's songs that
we can learn together.

♡ Playing fun music on a cassette player will help both of us:
bed time, before meal time, in the car, fussy time, company visiting time, etc.

I like to be silly.

It's OK to be silly
when you are little
and when you are
big. It makes life
more fun.

♡ You are my very best friend.

It's fun to use my imagination. I will be more creative if you encourage me.

Bunny
hop hop

Bird
flap your arms

Hide and Seek
(don't hide from
me too long)

Peek a Boo

arf! arf!

Dog

meow

Cat

Elephant
swing
your
trunk

Marching in a
Parade

Ring Around the Rosey

I like to pretend.
(I like you to
pretend with me)

I like to
play with
you.

Taking moments of time with me (silly playing, fun playing, reading to me and listening to me) shows me that YOU LOVE ME! When parents spend more time with their children, the result will be stronger, healthier children.

I like the library.

Don't forget to bring your library books back on time, and visit us often.

Remember the Librarian is here to help you.

There are so many new books we can take home because we use our library card. ♡ Don't forget to return our books on time and in good condition.

I like you to read to me often.

I like it when you point out colors and objects and make it special for me.
♡ Thank you

*If you can't read, you're not alone. Contact your local library or School District... they have special Adult Reading Programs.

I like to be taught to <u>LISTEN</u>.

to a bird

the wind

the cars

a baby crying

footsteps

soft music

raindrops

Did you know when I learn to *listen* I will do better when I go to school someday? Play this game with me: When I have learned to talk, teach me to "repeat" things you say. This is a very good way to learn listening skills. Show me "how to listen". Ask me to be very quiet and then we "listen" for special sounds.

I like weekends and holidays.

I like them because you play with me more and we aren't in a hurry.
Please don't watch too much TV or go shopping, golfing, adult playing or working all day.
I need some "fun" time with you.

I like animals.

It's fun for me to visit the park and zoo.
Thank you for protecting me from getting too close to the animals or possible danger.

I like my Mommy and my Daddy so much.

When we all live together we need to be nice to each other.
Please don't push me away when I need your hugs, or when I need you to "watch me" do something silly.
Your praise and acceptance (and Patience) makes me feel very important.

I like it when you talk to me with respect.

(especially when you understand that I am a small child)

Sweetheart - I will try hard to speak gently and to take more time to listen to you.

When you yell and get bossy and are always correcting me for every little thing, I feel discouraged and not very important.

Best of all I like BIG HUGS!

ONE HUG RULES

Infancy to 1 year old - 1 hug every hour
1 year to 2 years old - 1 hug every 1-2 hours
2 years to 3 years old - 1 hug every 2-3 hours
3 years old to 4 years old - 1 hug every 3-4 hours
4 years to 5 years old - 1 hug every 4-5 hours
5 years to 6 years old - 1 hug every 5-6 hours
6 years old to 100 years old -
At least a hug a day (or more)

♡ Thank you!

V. MY
THANK YOUS

Thank you for preparing my brother(s) and sister(s) for my coming home.

Please tell them that mostly I just sleep and cry and eat when I am little. But I will grow fast and then we can play.

*Even though new babies take a lot of your time, please don't forget the older children. These children may resist your hugs and compliments, but show your attention by : encouraging, praising, showing appreciation and showing your interest and concern daily. Have some "fun" with them, they will love you forever!

Thank you for teaching everyone how special it is to have a new baby.

It is nice to have a proud 'big' brother or sister who are kind and understanding,

Thank you for understanding the importance of taking time out for me.

Hugs at Bedtime

A Drive

Watch a Sunset

Reading Together

Talking Together

Ice Cream Store

Going for a Walk is nice too...

I learn more by seeing things and sharing them with you. I like your company.

I am learning to
LISTEN MORE & TALK LESS.
1. What did you learn today? (Pause & listen)
2. Did something funny happen?
Tell me about it. (Pause & listen)
3. Did you see any animals? (Pause & listen)
4. What was the weather like? (Pause & listen)

*As I TALK, just go along with my chatter.
(Don't finish my sentences).
Please look at me,
(it makes me feel loved).
Don't point out grammar
mistakes or imperfect
speech.*

Thank you for listening to me.

I like it when we talk about our day, our family, our friends. Ask me questions that will help me to think.

Sometimes I need only a few minutes of your time for you to simply "listen" to me. Thank you for showing respect for what I am trying to talk to you about. This is very important to me. When you listen I feel important and this is what helps my self esteem.

Thank you for finding subjects that help me to talk about many things.

Children who learn to express ideas and think, do better in school.
Please really "listen to me" and encourage me to express myself.
♡ Thank you.

Thank you for cooking healthful foods for me so my body can grow strong.

Fresh fruit and vegetables are better snacks than high sugar or fat foods.

We always wash our hands before we cook.

*Hint: When cleaning up: To discourage dangerous bacteria it is recommended to spray and clean all kitchen working surfaces with a disinfectant.

It's good for all of us to eat right and to be well.

Thank you for combing my hair.

Some children have
'tender heads' and need extra patience
when doing their hair.
Sometimes *'no-tangle'* conditioner
is helpful. Maybe you can cut
my hair shorter for easier
combing and brushing.

Thank you for washing my face.

When I am clean and well
groomed I feel good about myself.
(being clean helps
prevent disease)

Thank you for taking me to my checkups with the doctor and dentist.

1. We see the doctor for regular checkups.
2. We see the doctor when we are sick or injured.
3. When we see the doctor we should ask him questions so we can learn.

Turn back to page 27 for "questions" to ask the doctor or nurse.

Please learn how to do the Heimlich Maneuver & CPR. This can save lives.
(Consult a doctor or nurse soon about available classes.)

I am learning to brush my teeth.

Teach me to brush & floss everyday (morning and night) as soon as I have teeth.

♡ Please take me to a children's dentist when I am about 3 because this will teach us how to prevent tooth decay.

Thank you for letting me "do it myself" when I can.

Thank you for understanding that I need you to teach me to use my helping chart!

Allow me to make "choices": If I can tie my shoes at **5** years—let me!
If I want to make my bed at **3** years—encourage me!
Let me "CHOOSE" which clothes to wear, which socks to put on, which ribbons
for my hair, which healthful foods to eat, etc. (Give me a choice of
two things - I will choose one of them. This makes me feel SPECIAL)...
♡ It takes a little more time and more patience,
but I am learning to be responsible! Keep encouraging me!

Thank you for allowing me to be myself. Thank you for not "comparing" me to other children.

- If I am quiet and prefer to play alone sometimes – that's OK – that is the way I am.

We are special in our own special way.

- If I like to lead the way and make decisions – that's OK – I like being in charge.

- If I need friends and like to talk, chat and laugh – that's OK – I like being a close friend and helping others.

If I seem content and happy with my personality type – I'm OK.
But if I am quiet because I am depressed a lot or
aggressive because I am extra upset or angry,
then please check on me and get help for me if needed.

Thank you for letting me write letters, color & draw and write thank you notes to my Family and Friends.

When anyone sends me a card, money, or any kind of a gift,
teach me to always say "Thank-You" (notes are nice).
When I don't say thank-you people will think
I am rude & have poor manners.

Thank you for teaching me to remember birthdays and special occasions for my loved ones.

We can send cards or make a small gift.

Thank you for teaching me to share.

Sometimes this is hard for me to learn, so be patient with me.
(be a good example by sharing with others too)

*It helps children to have a snack area (cupboard, shelf, basket, drawer or something) where healthy snacks are available for the asking. When children ask for something, just send them to the "snack area" and they can pick a snack.

*Snacks do not replace breakfast, lunch and dinner. Snacks are helpful for in between regular meals.

Thank you for teaching me to respect our things and other people's property.

I don't want to grow up thinking it's OK to write on things (graffiti), or break things on purpose, make messes or do anything destructive! **PLEASE TEACH ME TO SHOW RESPECT!**

We are respectful.

Thank you for preparing and teaching me how to take care of our pets.

I am learning to take care of my pets!

Bathing and grooming, feeding, watering, and cleaning up after our pets will help me to learn to love and care for living things. Sometimes pets can be expensive because of food, care, and supplies. Please don't let a pet be a burden to our family's needs or interfere with our needs.

*Let us adopt a pet when our family is prepared for one.

Thank you for teaching me about money.

Please put some money in savings for me every month. This will help for college.

Piggy Bank

I will grow up faster than you think:

IF you respect money and plan every purchase - so will I,

IF you purchase only what we need - so will I,

IF you live within our means (and feel proud of it) - so will I,

IF you take care of our home, and all we have - so will I,

IF you don't cheat by buying things you don't really need - I won't either,

IF you set goals and always stay with the plan - so will I.

Thank you for being careful with our money.

We only buy what we need and we decide carefully about other purchases. (use charge cards with <u>caution</u> and try to put some money into savings)

*As I grow older, if I get everything I want (without earning it) I will soon not appreciate what I have. Working to earn something I want to purchase, will teach me how to value things.

WE PAY OUR BILLS ON TIME:
Rent & Phone
Electric - Heat & Water
Credit Expenses, Car & Insurance

B A N K

Thank you for teaching me how to behave in stores and other public places.

1. Be sure I am rested and fed.
2. Take a snack along.
3. Never allow me to run around, touch things, or be too loud. Take my Wanderless™ or something that will help me not to wander.

♡ Do not leave me in the toy area of a store while you shop. This is wrong. Children are NOT supposed to play with new toys that a store is trying to sell.
Also, children should remain with their parents at all times.
It is neglectful and dangerous to leave children alone.
♡ Do NOT open packages of food, candy or gum and eat them before paying for them. This is not a good example for children.

WOW! Well-behaved children!

Thank you for not taking me to some public places until I am old enough.

It's not fair for the rest of us to listen to screaming or crying children.

Most of the time young children should be left with a caretaker when parents go to movies, theatres, fine restaurants, and most stores.

Thank you for being considerate whenever you go anywhere.

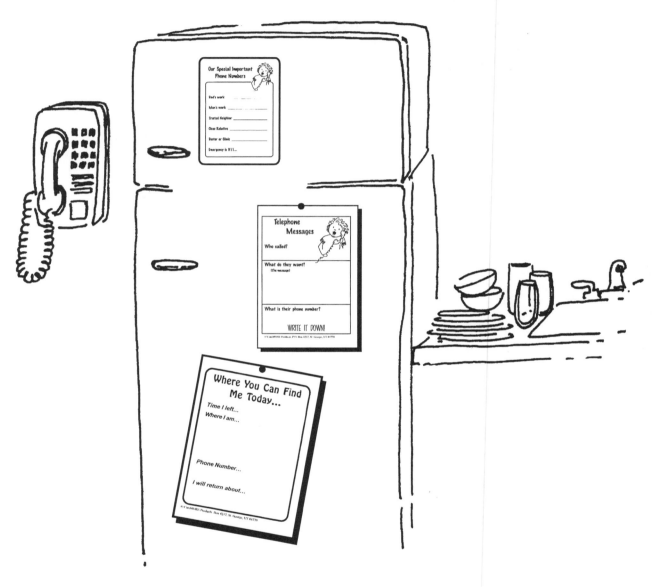

Knowing where everyone is and having important phone numbers handy, makes everyone more secure.
*It is a way of showing family respect.

Thank you for teaching me to not go anywhere with anyone unless you say it's OK.

♡ Teach me not to look at strangers or talk to them - NO MATTER WHAT. Show me how to SCREAM NO!! and run and tell someone fast. (family)

Hey, little boy–do you want some candy and a ride home?

I have been taught to play where I can always see my mom!

Teach me my area code ___ ___ ___
and phone number ___ ___ ___ ___ - ___ ___ ___ ___

Please teach me by asking me many questions. There are other ways someone may try to get me to go with them.

EXAMPLES

* Hey Kid, can you help me find my dog?
* Do you know where the hamburger place is?
* Come with me. Your mother is sick and she sent me to get you.

How am I answering the questions?

Keep teaching me!

_____

Teach me to ALWAYS tell someone and to run away from strange cars and people who make me feel confused and worried! REMEMBER, NEVER ALLOW ME TO BE OUT OF YOUR SIGHT. CHECK ON ME OFTEN. YOU NEED TO ALWAYS WATCH ME BECAUSE I AM LITTLE.
You need to watch me because I am little.
♡ Thank you

Thank you for driving me to daycare and other places.

♡ Please talk to me as we drive and point out interesting things along the way.

Drive safely and please remember to BUCKLE UP seat belts and car seats.

Hint: Keep snacks, small toys, water, baby formula, diapers and wipes in the car.

"Thank you" for being smart. Smart parents plan ahead and know how to take care of their cars which saves money (and stress):

*Buy gasoline when the car is no lower then ¼ tank (Don't risk running out of gas).

*Have the oil and filter changed every 3,000 miles (the car will have fewer repairs).

*Know about power steering and transmissions fluid, lubing, etc. and when they may be needed.

*Have the tires rotated. (If you aren't sure, "ask" a car expert.)

*Wash our car about once a week (a clean car makes us all feel better). Vacuuming is good too!

*Don't allow messy foods or drinks in the car. "Clean up" can create a problem and added stresses.

*Teach me to RESPECT our car and our home. (We can eat our bigger meals in a restaurant or at home.)

Thank you for finding help for me or for you if anyone has a disability.

Please use the support services and agencies that can help us.
(ask the Doctor, the Clinic, or the Health Department)

I know my limitations are extra work for you, but I am so glad you are my parent. As time goes on we will both do better.
Thank you for your encouragement and trust.
I need you...

Thank you for your patience.

♡ REMEMBER to take a break once in awhile. I will be OK with a trusted friend or relative.

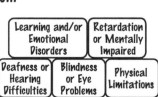

| Learning and/or Emotional Disorders | Retardation or Mentally Impaired |
| Deafness or Hearing Difficulties | Blindness or Eye Problems | Physical Limitations |

Thank you for saying "I'm sorry" when you are wrong.

Everyone makes mistakes. You can help me to understand how to say I'm sorry when I make a mistake.

Some adults need to practice saying "I'm Sorry"... (The more you say it, the easier it is to do it. This helps to mend hurt feelings and develop respect.)

I'm sorry for......

Thank you for not labeling me with bad names.

These names should be said often.

These names are not nice when they are said in mean and hurtful ways.

kind
sweet smart
helpful
generous
angel
caring

dumb
mean
lazy
selfish
slow
brat
stupid

None of us is perfect but we need to be told everything positive about ourselves, and <u>please compliment me often.</u>

Thank you for understanding if I have a need for Pre-School, Nursery, Montessori, Head-Start, etc.

(even a couple of days a week will prepare me)

Sometimes before I go to Kindergarten I need to learn from others and prepare for real school.

*WARNING
Sometimes other children (or me) act mean (bullies). This can happen all the way through high school. Please teach me to tell you, tell the teacher, and tell my friends whenever someone is being mean or saying mean things. Also, if I show aggressive behaviors, please observe me and help me so I won't hurt others.

Thank you for all the nice things you do for me.

I like to go to bed at about the same time every night.
I love to hear happy house sounds while I fall asleep.
Routines and limits make me feel secure.
Sometimes I may be afraid of the dark.
A small night light (and a story and sweet hugs) are helpful. I may also be afraid of Bad Dreams, so if I have a nightmare please talk to me and help me understand it is not real.

♡ Thank you

Thank you for reading this special book. We will understand each other better and know there are answers for lots of things.

Thank you for loving children. Maris Foss Hafen

Dear Mommy Dear Daddy

Love at Home

♡ We are very lucky because we have each other.

VI. HELP ME

This section is to teach me how to
mind the rules inside and outside our home.

Help me because I am little.

I need to "learn" how to control myself, "learn" that my choices have
consequences and "learn" the rules of our home, the school and the community.
You are my teacher and my example.

Help me by setting limits for me.

- **Bedtime**
- **Playtime**
- **TV Time**
- **Time Out** (when I misbehave)

Setting limits helps me to take control of myself.
(I don't have the maturity or skills to do this - I need you)

MY LIMITS
(Make me feel secure)

BATHTIME
Set a time ....

BEDTIME
Set a time ....

TANTRUMS ....

(crying yelling, saying NO)

Remove to another area and firmly tell me I can return when I am under control.

INTERRUPTING CONVERSATIONS ....

I don't mean to interrupt but teach me to be patient while you finish talking. (Don't take too long)

Help me by not tolerating too much sulking and pouting.

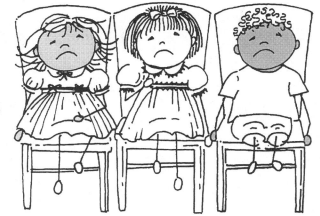

I am learning things can't go MY way all the time.
*Remember, my little feelings are very important. Calmly talk to me about my anger or sadness so I can understand how to handle my feelings.

This habit can get worse with age. (Getting away with too much sulking and pouting can lead to a selfish personality.)

Help me not to bite, pinch, or hit other people.

When you hear crying or screaming, please don't react with yelling, yanking, or slapping > please ask questions, listen, and teach.

It is wrong to hurt people or animals.

<u>What you expect of me becomes "real" to me.</u>
- Do you <u>expect</u> me to share or to be a bully?
- Do you <u>expect</u> me to be mean or to be a nice person?
- Do you <u>expect</u> me to be bossy or to be polite?
- Do you <u>expect</u> me to ignore you (and the rules) or to listen and pay attention?

Toys

Help me by setting rules that fit my age and ability.

If I try to do things before I am ready I can become confused and frustrated. These feelings can lead to anger and unhappiness. Please don't expect too much from me, but allow me to do things I am comfortable with.

*If I am two, don't expect me to do what a five year old can do. If I am five, don't compare me to a seven year old. Be reasonable. Be understanding.

Help me by not ignoring me when I misbehave in public.

Ignoring me (especially in public) gives me permission to keep doing naughty things (and I will just get worse) I NEED YOU to set limits.

(Remove me from a public place if you have to)

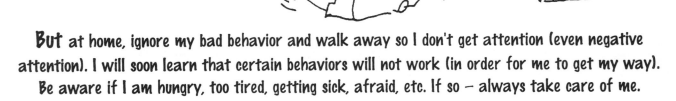

But at home, ignore my bad behavior and walk away so I don't get attention (even negative attention). I will soon learn that certain behaviors will not work (in order for me to get my way). Be aware if I am hungry, too tired, getting sick, afraid, etc. If so – always take care of me.

Help me by being consistent.

1. **Consistent means to plan ahead.**
   (make a plan for our house rules)

2. **Consistent means you stick to the plan** (rules) **the best you can.**

3. **Consistent means not changing the plan** (rules) **from one day to the next.**

4. **Consistent means sticking to the plan** (rules) **outside the home as well as at home.**

   (children sometimes test us more in public places but we still have to be fair and firm.)

People appreciate parents who do not tolerate out of control children.

* Take time to allow your child to talk about their "feelings". Discover if something has happened to them or is bothering them. (Maybe they are resisting the rules because they need to talk to you and they need your comfort or reassurance.) LISTEN CAREFULLY.
* If they state they don't like the rules, simply tell them when you were young you didn't like them sometimes too, but they are still the rules.
* While children are learning the rules, they MUST feel your love and support. LISTEN TO WHAT THEY ARE FEELING (not just what they tell you). Being an understand parent creates strong families.

Help me to have respect for others when I am in a car.

It is not safe for a driver to have fighting, screaming children in a car. **STOP THE CAR** if you need to! (Keep some books and small toys and little snacks in the car.)

♡ Thank You

Car airbag tests have shown it is best to buckle up children in the back seat. Activated airbags may harm a child.

Help me to solve conflicts peacefully.

I need to learn how to get along with people in our home
so I will know how to behave with my friends.

When children misbehave, many times it is best to give them a "TIME OUT" from each other until they decide they are ready to be nicer. Sometimes the child is tired or coming down with a cold (etc.) and they are a little "grumpy". If so, respect their alone time and have the other children keep their distance for awhile.

(This helps everyone...)

* Help me to discuss ways I can solve problems:
Instead of grabbing the toy I could _____
Instead of screaming I could _____
Instead of hitting I could _____
Instead of being bossy I could _____
When I learn to "problem solve" (find solutions), I will be less of a problem.
* Make sure my solutions are safe, will make the other person feel OK, and will make me feel OK.

Help me to not pick up or touch everything when we are shopping

*I need to also be respectful in other people's homes.

Help me to respect all things...

Most people work very hard to have nice homes, office buildings, schools and neighborhoods. I have no business doing bad things to property. IT IS WRONG. If I harm anyone's property, PLEASE teach me to find a way to fix it. (Example: Go to the person and admit the wrong; Do chores around the house to earn money to pay for it, etc.)

♡ Thank you for teaching me to be an honest and responsible person.

95

Help me by being firm but fair.

This gives me a feeling of safety and security. Thank you for setting limits.

Help me by watching me BUT...
give me space to explore.

It is important to get outside and enjoy nature. Let's learn about bugs and butterflies and birds and plants and trees and...

Children have delicate skin. Make sure they have sunscreen on when you take them outside. (Check with your doctor)

Help me by watching other successful parents.

(be willing to change...)
You can learn
from others...

Sense of humor...
enjoys children

Not too over protective
or too strict

Relaxed...but
responsible

Speaks kindly,
not too bossy

Have some fun once in a while...find a reliable caretaker.
• Find a Family Support Center in your area. Meeting other parents and
learning new ideas is not only "fun", but can be a life saver for you... This is a
nice way to discover your child and to appreciate his/her personality and traits.

Help me by teaching me table manners.

When I am young I can learn to eat carefully if my food is cut in small pieces. I need you to help me. Please don't get angry if I spill—I try hard.

Hint:
- Use a smaller plastic glass for me.
- Pour ⅓ into my glass (at a time).
- Use a non-spill cup with a drink lid.
- Be cautious about using glass. Serious accidents can happen & injure a child.

Remember – accidents happen to everyone. <u>Please</u> be understanding.

Help me by understanding when something is an accident.

Most things are accidents (please be patient and teach me).

...But when I do things on purpose (that are damaging) I need you to be more firm so I can learn to be respectful of people's property.

♡ Please be a consistent parent by sticking to our House Rules.
Repeat the rules and use TIME OUT when necessary.

Help me by complimenting me when I do things right.

Thank you for helping me! You did a good job!

If you tell me the good things about myself I will want to keep doing things that are good.

Help me by being loving and caring, BUT...

Sometimes handicaps, health problems, divorce, etc. can be an excuse for me to misbehave. When you continually feel sorry for me and allow repeated out-of-control behaviors (study this chapter) I can develop a poor self-image from misbehaving so much. Please be understanding and kind and considerate as you teach me.

Help me by remembering that YOU are my parent.

I like my grandma, my grandpa, my relatives, my babysitter......
BUT YOU are my parent and YOU are responsible for me.

Help me to play in SAFE areas.

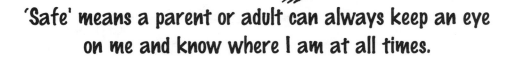

'Safe' means a parent or adult can always keep an eye on me and know where I am at all times.

Help me by not being overpermissive.

(don't let me do things I should not be doing!)

I am learning to mind the rules.

Time Out Room

I SHOULD NOT...
1. hurt people or animals
2. destroy other people's stuff
3. get into other people's things
4. yell & scream & run through houses or stores

Place the child where you can see him/her. Let the child know you are giving him/her a few minutes to "think". One to five minutes is a long time for a child. Set the timer so you won't forget to go to your child and talk it out.

Don't let my bad behavior wear you down. You are my parents and I need you to be firm and <u>consistent</u>. When we "talk things out", please LISTEN to me as I tell-you-my-feelings. (Don't "you" do all of the talking.)

I will learn more if I can tell you HOW: "I can control myself next time", or "Instead of hitting I will talk to my friend", or "Instead of screaming & yelling I will talk reasonably", etc. Take at least 3 minutes or more (if needed) to help me talk about how I can-change-my-behaviors then "compliment" me on how I am making better choices. The more you take TIME to listen and help me, the less I will be out-of-control as I grow older.

*NEVER put a child in a closet for punishment.

Help me by keeping rules and limits yourself.

You are my best example.
I am always watching you because
I want to grow up and be like you.
♡ Thank You

Mom and Dad Do's

Orderly Home ✓
Healthy Habits ✓
Exercise ✓
Obey Traffic Laws ✓
Honest ✓
Kind ✓

P.S.

It's OK when you make a
mistake or have a bad day
once in a while.
I love you and I understand.
Don't get discouraged.
It takes lots of practice
to be a parent.

VII. CHANGES AND HARD STUFF

A. Emergencies & Disasters

B. Sickness & Accidents

C. Divorce & Separation

D. Dating & New Relationships

E. Abuse

F. Personal Challenges

Dear Mommy and Daddy,
When you have to do something new,
do you feel SCARED and NERVOUS?

I DO TOO!

My Stuff

Dishes

Bowls

Clothes

Putting everything
in boxes makes me worried.

If we have to move, I would feel better if you could put my things in a special
box so I could see they are safe. (toy, blanket, book, change of clothes, snack)
I need you to tell me everything will be OK!
♡ Thank You

FLASH FLOODS, LIGHTNING, SERIOUS HEAT WAVE,

A. Sometimes there are EMERGENCIES and DISASTERS

Dear Mommy and Daddy,
Floods, earthquakes, etc. and other hard stuff happens all the time.

We need to be prepared and have a 72 hour kit for each member of our family.
♡ Thank You

When emergencies happen - please try to be prepared.

1. Learn how to shut off the gas, electricity, and water. (this could help save our home)

2. Keep a container somewhere in the house that has emergency supplies that will help us for at least 72 hours.
   Suggestions:
   - Flashlight
   - Shoes, extra clothing
   - Water, juices, drinks
   - Food: granola bars, crackers, dried fruit, cookies, dehydrated soup mixes, chocolate mix, powdered fruit drink and foods for baby, etc.
   - Toilet paper or kleenex, diapers
   - First aid supplies: bandaids and antibiotic ointment, any prescription medicines
   - Toothpaste, toothbrush, bar of soap
   - Blanket and towel

   *Favorite toy, coloring book and crayons, paper, pencil

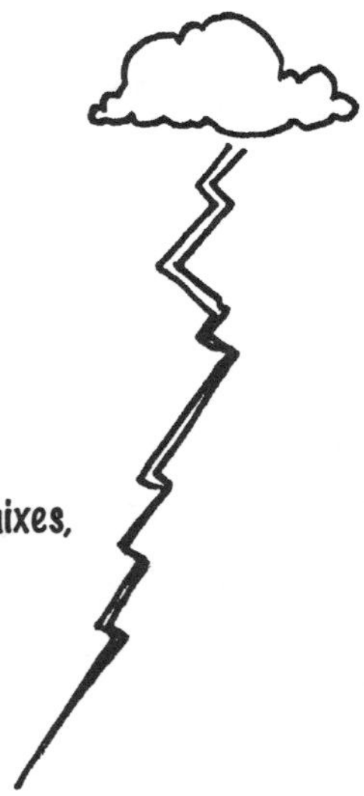

3. Note: Sweets help to reduce stress - they have a temporary calming effect.

4. Add additional supplies according to the needs of your family.

RIOTS, FIRE, FAMILY DISASTER, EARTHQUAKES, TORNADOES, FREEZING

SERIOUS HEAT WAVE, FLASH FLOODS, LIGHTNING,

EARTHQUAKES, TORNADOES, HURRICANES, SEVERE FREEZING TEMPERATURES

FIRE and BURNS

* Did you know over 2 million people are BURNED each year?

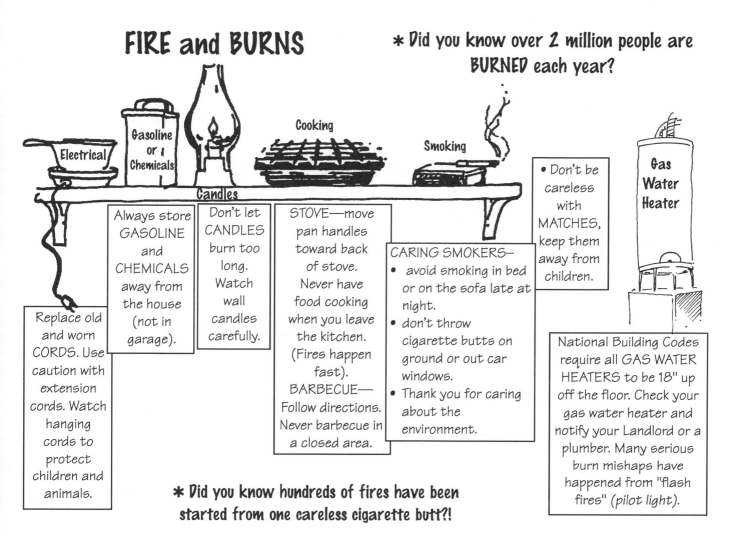

Electrical

Gasoline or Chemicals

Candles

Cooking

Smoking

Gas Water Heater

Replace old and worn CORDS. Use caution with extension cords. Watch hanging cords to protect children and animals.

Always store GASOLINE and CHEMICALS away from the house (not in garage).

Don't let CANDLES burn too long. Watch wall candles carefully.

STOVE—move pan handles toward back of stove. Never have food cooking when you leave the kitchen. (Fires happen fast). BARBECUE—Follow directions. Never barbecue in a closed area.

CARING SMOKERS—
• avoid smoking in bed or on the sofa late at night.
• don't throw cigarette butts on ground or out car windows.
• Thank you for caring about the environment.

• Don't be careless with MATCHES, keep them away from children.

National Building Codes require all GAS WATER HEATERS to be 18" up off the floor. Check your gas water heater and notify your Landlord or a plumber. Many serious burn mishaps have happened from "flash fires" (pilot light).

* Did you know hundreds of fires have been started from one careless cigarette butt?!

PREVENTION and TREATMENT

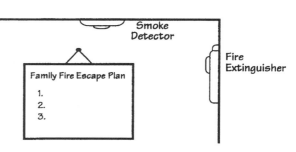

Smoke Detector

Fire Extinguisher

Family Fire Escape Plan
1.
2.
3.

✓ Smoke detectors for the house.
✓ Fire extinguisher for kitchen.
✓ Fire escape plan for the family (practice!).
• Show plan to babysitter.

1. **Little burn** Use cold water immediately (not ice). Keep burned area in cold water at least 15 minutes. Cover with bandage, don't break blister, let it heal. If needed, give pain medicine made for children (not aspirin).

2. **Serious burn** Apply cold water, and call a doctor or go to an emergency room. Keep burned area in a cold wet towel or continue to spray with cold water until you see the doctor.

3. **'On fire' burn!** Smother the burn fast! NEVER run. Roll or wrap up in something to stop the flame. Continue to spray cold water on burned areas while you go to hospital or while you call 911! *Do not put butter or any cream on the burn. *Do not pull off any burned skin.

Anytime someone gets burned it is very scary.
You must try to remain calm because you need to put out the fire and cool the skin.
*Remember to check Smoke Detectors, Carbon Monoxide Detector and Fire Extinguishers once a year. (Try Labor Day.)

B. Sometimes there are ACCIDENTS and SICKNESS

* Check on me often. Sick or injured people need extra attention.
* Stay with me when I am sick. Cancel your plans - I need you more than ever when I'm not feeling well.
* If I have the flu or a similar sickness, do not take me out. (It is not good for me or fair to others.)

Sometimes foods don't taste as good to me, so popcicles, juices, puddings,
some cereals, certain soups, and other foods that aren't too spicy will be appreciated.
♡ Thank you.

If someone I love goes away to a hospital for a long time, I need to know what is happening.
(Just tell me the basics)

I don't understand illness but I will feel better if you talk to me and explain things.
You don't need to tell me the details, because I may be too little to understand and it will worry me too much. Just tell me the basics and keep telling me "we will be OK"...

There are many kinds of hurts & illness. (or death)

When there is

Please tell me

1. A little hurt
(earache, small
cut, etc.)

"It will get better soon. Let me help make it better." (drops for ears, ointment for scratch, etc.)

*If it is a cut, stop the bleeding by pressing on the cut. When bleeding stops, wash gently with cold water. Carefully use a mild soap if the cut is dirty. Cover with an adhesive bandage and keep the cut clean. (Change old bandage as needed.)

* If you cannot stop a nosebleed, call 911, or an Emergency Clinic.

2. A big hurt
(broken bone,
flu, serious rash)

> If you are upset and these instructions seem too complicated, do your best while you go to the hospital or call 911.

"We will see the doctor and he will help you get better." (Talk to the child on the way to a doctor. Keep reassuring him/her that the doctor knows just what to do, and it will be better soon.) On your way to a doctor try to do the following:
* If it is a big cut, cover with clean cloth. Press down hard.
  Do not take cloth away from the cut. If the cloth get full of blood, wrap a new cloth over the old one.
  Keep pressing for at least 5 minutes. Check clock.
· When bleeding stops, put tape over cloth. You will know when the bleeding stops because the cloth won't fill up with blood. Wind tape over cloth - Make it a little tight, but not too tight.
· If possible, raise feet, but not if the person's head is injured. If a cut is on arm or leg, raise it so it is higher than person's chest. You can put 2 or 3 pillows under the feet. (Keep the person warm.) Can use a blanket.
* For poisoning, call 911 or Poison Control Center. Tell WHAT and HOW MUCH the person swallowed. Tell person's AGE and WEIGHT. Try to tell HOW LONG AGO person swallowed the poison. Save the bottle.

3. Serious illness or accident

"Sometimes people get very sick and go to hospitals for some time. Most people get well and are happy to come home."

I am little and I don't understand death or funerals.
If you choose to take me to the funeral, please prepare me.
(Don't shut the child out, stay close, hold him often and listen.)

1.   It is usually very quiet and peaceful. (It depends on the culture)
2.   Some people will be very sad and might be crying.
3.   Sometimes they show the person's body in a casket.
4.   Some people kiss the dead person good-bye, but please don't force me to do this. (Ask me if I want to).
5.   All of this is very confusing and upsetting to me.

♡ Please be understanding and stay close to me.

C. Sometimes there is
DIVORCE OR SEPARATION

Try to do all you can to NOT have a divorce.

- Be Honest with one another. (Express feelings - not anger)
- Be Considerate and Respectful toward one another. (Be less selfish)
- Manage money wisely. (Discuss all money matters together)
- Avoid drugs, alcohol, gambling and pornography
- Show integrity by controlling your thoughts and actions. (Self-control)
- Never flirt or have an affair with someone. (Seek counseling instead)
- If you think you are attracted to someone else, practice thinking about the many good things in your husband or wife & children. (Over & over again) You will discover how wonderful your family is.
- Do NOT say negative things about one another to others. (Stop feeling sorry for yourself)
- Learn what "love" really is. (What do you respect & admire?)
- Seek counseling early - Stop Blaming - Be willing to see both sides
- Do more together as a family. (Have some fun!)
- The longer you are married the stronger your love can grow (if both husband and wife are sincerely trying). It is worth it!
- But if you are being abused - seek help immediately!

Dear Mommy and Daddy,
No matter what happened, I'm too little.

I DON'T UNDERSTAND why you don't like each other anymore.
I still like BOTH of you!

PLEASE Don't keep telling me bad things about each other.

No matter how old I get,
I will NEVER want to hear bad things about you from each other.

Because of the divorce & the changes, Sometimes I feel......

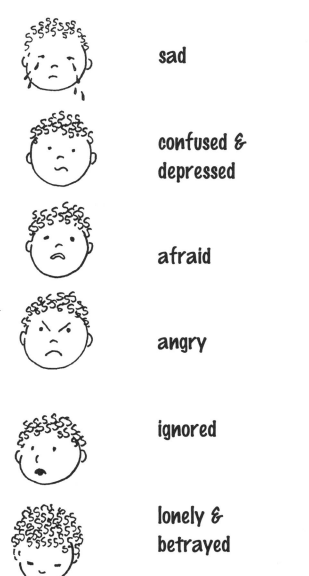

sad

confused & depressed

afraid

angry

ignored

lonely & betrayed

I'm not myself with all these new people and places in my life.

REMEMBER, I feel what you feel...

Sometimes you seem......

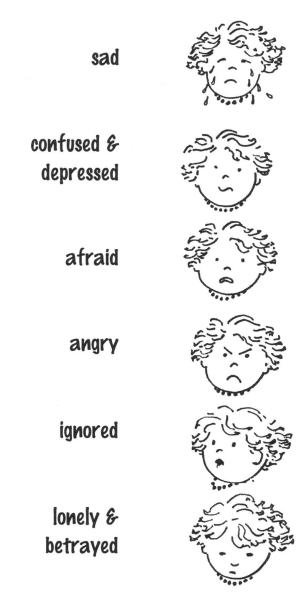

sad

confused & depressed

afraid

angry

ignored

lonely & betrayed

I can tell this must be very hard for you too. You aren't quite the same anymore either.

I can tell that you are sometimes ANGRY.

I am so glad we were told to go to DIVORCE FAMILY COUNSELING. We need to ALL understand how we can continue to be a family and adjust to the many changes.

Mom & Dad, Please work on letting go of your anger toward one another.

This is the one way you can help all of us to heal from this pain.

• Remember - your child's needs should be #1.

I can tell you sometimes want to GET EVEN.

But it won't do any good. Everyone has to figure things out. <u>Please</u> let it go.

Letting go of the Past

Letting go of anger

Looking toward the Future

Attend a divorce workshop for families
• Learn about what children of divorce go through.

• Learn what happens to the children when divorced parents constantly put one another down.

• Learn about brainwashing and the damage it does.

• Learn about being a step parent and the damage that is done when the child's parent is criticized.

• Learn how to "<u>work together</u>" to do what is the best for each child.

• Be unselfish • Be Responsible • Be Adult

I know you have many needs.

Loneliness
Wanting someone to care
Wanting someone to help
Needing understanding
Needing enough money, etc.

? ? ? ? ?

Caution: For most people it takes two to four years to adjust after a divorce.

It looks like we're both going through a lot of the same things.

Family Center

But I am LITTLE and I need you to help us find the answers.

I STILL LOVE "BOTH" OF YOU!!

Do keep LOVING ME so I don't feel like you'll leave me too. ALWAYS tell me you will never leave me and that you will always return when you leave for work (or anywhere). For many months; I will need to hear your reassurance over and over again.

PLEASE REMEMBER I love my grandmas and grandpas very much.

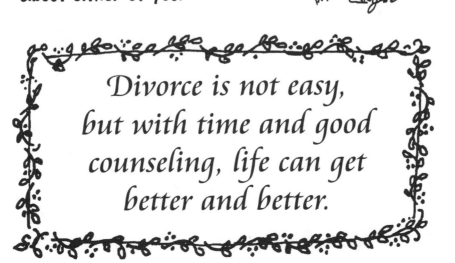

If my grandparents want to be a part of my life, please don't make them go away or not let them see me because you're angry with each other.
It makes my little heart ache.
They are special to me, but please teach them to also not tell me bad things about either of you.

> *Divorce is not easy, but with time and good counseling, life can get better and better.*

D. Dating, New Relationships, Remarriage

Dating means getting to know someone.

Be very careful when you begin dating. Be careful about partying too much, drinking too much and being involved sexually. Remember you are my Mommy (or Daddy) and I don't want you to leave me too often, or to do things that are not safe.

• No one should be more important than your child.

♡ *Choose the best. You marry who you date.*

Remember you're doing this for all of us.

My Dad wants the best for me.

My Mom makes good choices.

Please be smart in your choices. Do your homework.
♡ Good luck.

Dear Mommy & Daddy,
When you are dating ......
Please look past the surface!!!

- Do they like children? Do they include your children in activities?
- Are they kind to all people…waiters, attendants, people who serve you?
- Do they have a temper or excessive moodiness or extreme silence? Do they have to always be "right" and not listen to or respect your opinion?
- Are they willing to talk about their feelings honestly?
- Are they on their own? Or do they live off of other people?
- Do they have a good job that can support a family? Do they have many debts? Do they blame others or make excuses for their bad debts?
- Do they pay all of their bills? Do they handle money & charge cards wisely?
- Can they be trusted? Have they borrowed and paid it back?
- Do they follow through with what they say? (promises, commitments, etc.)
- How long have they been divorced? Did they attend a Divorce Family Workshop? Is their child (children) number one in their life?
- Do they pay their child support regularly? (If they have children).
- Do they expect "favors" because you dated them? Is too much expected?
- Do they have any bad habits? (drugs, alcohol, swearing, gambling, pornography, etc.)
- Are they unselfish? Do they sincerely help others (often) who have problems or need assistance? Do they share? Are they helpful toward family?
- Are they willing to give up something they always do for something you would rather do? (showing unselfishness) Is appreciation shown?
- Are they extremely jealous or possessive or flirty with others around you? (This is selfishness) Do they "check up" on you often and try to control you?
- Do they find fault with you or criticize you often? (This is a form of control) CAUTION: Do you feel you have to apologize for being yourself? Are you always trying to please? Do you feel you need to ask permission when you want to do something?
- Do they share your standards? If you choose to take the "higher road" do they respect your choice or belittle you? (Read this list again.)

 BE CAREFUL!

E. Sometimes there are abusive people.

There are many kinds of ABUSE.

1. **Emotional:** lashing out about everything OR ignoring and neglecting the child or overindulging (doing too much and not setting limits). The child is confused at what the parent expects.

2. **Verbal:** constantly putting a child or the family down, extreme anger, or bad swearing (not being a nice person). The child is afraid to share feelings or talk about personal interests.

3. **Financial:** making a child suffer because money is not being earned or managed properly (saying that the child costs too much or child has to go without the basics: clothes, food, or fun). Child feels guilty when things are done for him.

4. **Physical:** yanking, pulling, slapping, hurting, hitting, and taking anger out on a child. Child begins to feel he is bad and deserves abuse - sometimes into adulthood.

5. **Sexual:** touching a child anywhere around his panty area, or any adult forcing a child to touch or look at his or her private parts, talking sexual, or showing pornography (movies, magazines). This is horrible!

♡I was not born to be abused in any way.

Over 90% of abuse victims are women
(and many children.)

Mommy—please tell someone—or get some help! I am always afraid.

*Women who abuse should also be reported.

There are safe places

Everytime you allow yourself to be yelled at, put down (criticized), pushed, shoved or hit—

it feels like it is happening to me —I hurt and I am very scared.
I worry about you (& me) all the time.

Thank you Mommy

Please do something (family violence centers, child protection centers, counseling, etc.) Call your Local Health Department, Police Department or 911

Sometimes friends and relatives do *secret abuse.*

(Be careful who you leave me with)

Please watch my moods and sleep patterns.
Talk to me a lot, so I can feel safe to talk to you.

Dear Mommy and Daddy,
Teach me not to be afraid to tell you if something bad happens to me.

Thank you for taking me seriously, but please don't become loud and angry. Be gentle and patient with me, then go to the source who hurt me and press charges against them (away from me, not in my presence). Leave me with a trusted friend or relative if you need to take action quickly.

Thank you for teaching me to be careful about my body.

This is "MY" body
⟷
I am the owner

When I have grown out of diapers PLEASE teach me to NEVER let anyone try to touch me around my panty or shorts or bathing suit area of my body.
Teach me to say NO! and tell you.

If you know someone who is harming a child in a very bad way (ABUSE), please DON'T IGNORE IT!

REPORT IT!
You may be that child's only hope. (if you are the one doing it — get help so you will stop hurting children!)

Any kind of ABUSE is serious.

If your parents did any of the following it was wrong. You DO NOT need to repeat this behavior.
Things are passed down from generation to generation, please be the one who will STOP bad behaviors.
Each generation should try to make the next generation better.

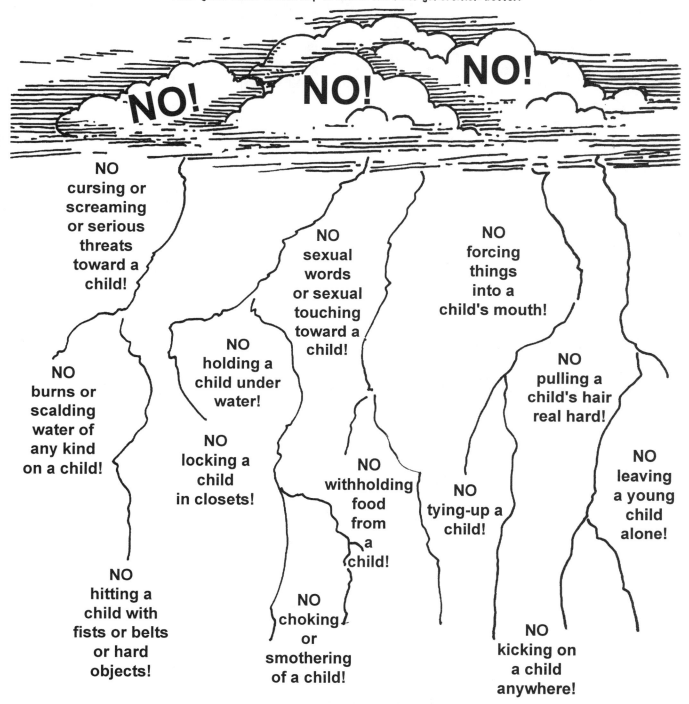

NO! NO! NO!

NO cursing or screaming or serious threats toward a child!

NO sexual words or sexual touching toward a child!

NO forcing things into a child's mouth!

NO burns or scalding water of any kind on a child!

NO holding a child under water!

NO pulling a child's hair real hard!

NO locking a child in closets!

NO withholding food from a child!

NO leaving a young child alone!

NO tying-up a child!

NO hitting a child with fists or belts or hard objects!

NO choking or smothering of a child!

NO kicking on a child anywhere!

*Remember, this is NOT discipline, this is abuse.
*Please read pages 90-102 again. With practice and help from others we can be a happy & strong family.

Please don't be afraid to get help! Please listen to the counselors! Please care about me! (us)

119

STOP!!

Before you lose control and hurt me badly ......

1. Quickly go to another room.
2. Step outside & "think" — calm down your anger.
3. Call a relative.

   Keep their phone numbers handy.
4. Call a friend or a church leader.
5. Last resort - call 911.

DON'T DAMAGE ME!

Going TOO FAR means
the punishment is too cruel (too mean) for the problem.

Love
means
feeling
Safe

F. Sometimes we have other PERSONAL CHALLENGES

*(depression, loneliness, food or eating disorders,
alcohol and drugs, gambling and other bad habits.)
There is always hope and help.*

When you are a parent sometimes you can feel isolated.

It's nice to have some good friends with children
too. It helps to talk things out. Call the closest
school about parenting classes.

If you feel overwhelmed all the time by any of the following, PLEASE GET HELP!

(GET HELP means to call a doctor, a church leader, counselor, etc.)

1. **Mood Swings** (highs and lows)
2. **Always blaming others**
3. **Anger** (out of control)
4. **Depression** (can't get out of bed)
5. **Isolation** (not wanting anything to do with family, friends, or support groups)
6. **Negative about everyone and everything.**

♡ You will help me by helping yourself.

Thank you for not smoking or drinking or doing drugs.

I want you to live a long, long life.
You are so special to me!
I know you don't want me
to have these habits.
(Bad habits are hard on everyone)

Bad habits are hard on families.

Alcohol
Drugs
Gambling
Food Disorders
Smoking

Please get help so you can teach me _not_ to do these things...

♡ I get confused and scared when you are out of control.
Please get help and counseling for any obsession or addiction.

I know it's hard to recognize that we have some of these problems (DENIAL)

Please take an honest look at your behaviors. Everything you do affects me.

★ If you live with someone who has these behaviors, please get counseling for our family.
We need help as much as the addict.

VIII. Grandma's Favorite Hints

Dear Children,
Here are some of our
favorite hints for......
1. Household Hints
2. Family Meals
3. Treasure Chest of Hints
Love,
Grandma Marie

Do a Daily Check before the day has begun:

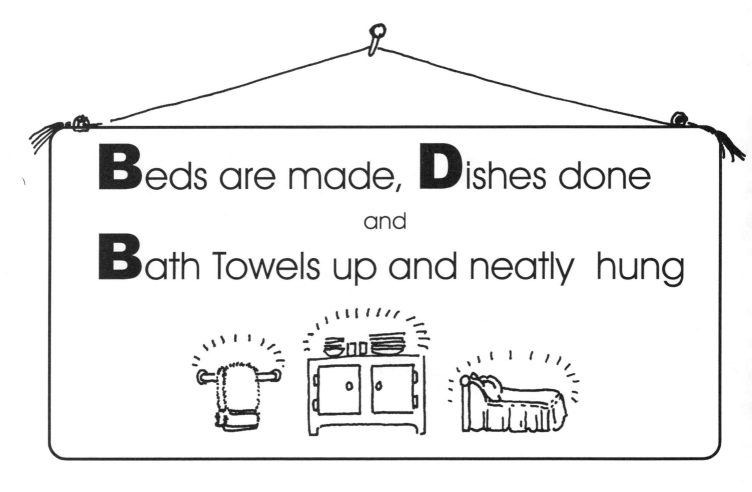

Beds are made, **D**ishes done

and

Bath Towels up and neatly hung

A little bit of order is better than none at all.

If you have more time, do more.

Remember, your home should make everyone feel good.

(Continual messes do not feel good)

1. HOUSE

The next few pages are going to show you the "basics" for cleaning a house, shopping, preparing food and meal planning....

See the plan:

- Clutter Fixers
- Leap through the Laundry
- Attack the Kitchen
- Breeze through the Bedrooms
- Brighten the Bathrooms
- Weekly Magic
- House Rules

THE HOUSE HINTS

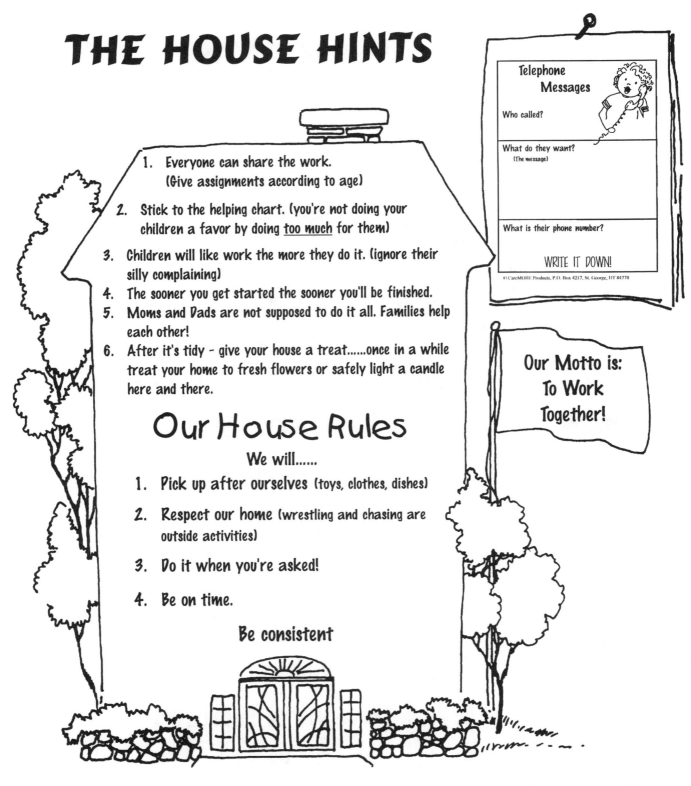

Telephone Messages

Who called?

What do they want?
(The message)

What is their phone number?

WRITE IT DOWN!

© CareMORE Products, P.O. Box 4217, St. George, UT 84770

1. Everyone can share the work.
   (Give assignments according to age)

2. Stick to the helping chart. (you're not doing your children a favor by doing <u>too much</u> for them)

3. Children will like work the more they do it. (ignore their silly complaining)

4. The sooner you get started the sooner you'll be finished.

5. Moms and Dads are not supposed to do it all. Families help each other!

6. After it's tidy - give your house a treat......once in a while treat your home to fresh flowers or safely light a candle here and there.

Our House Rules

We will......

1. Pick up after ourselves (toys, clothes, dishes)

2. Respect our home (wrestling and chasing are outside activities)

3. Do it when you're asked!

4. Be on time.

Be consistent

Our Motto is:
To Work
Together!

Your home will be happier if you take telephone messages for one another!

When your children are old enough to answer the phone they should be taught to be polite to callers.

Teach them to take messages. (The telephone is not a toy)

How fast do you want your house clean?

(if you really move quickly you can do it in less than one hour!)

All you need is a plan...

1. Wake up, get dressed, comb your hair, make your bed, feed the family.

2. Decide what to have for dinner by 10 a.m. (before you go to work or start your day) Start crockpot, put frozen meats in fridge to thaw, or write grocery list, etc.

3. To begin: take the phone off the hook, don't turn on TV.

4. Set the timer for 45 minutes (if you need extra motivation)

5. Race or sprint through the house and pick up clutter.

6. Put the clutter in the room where it belongs......work smart!

p.s. Adjust the plan to your individual working schedule.

Where does the clutter go?

1. Trash can or trash bags
2. Laundry hamper or basket
3. Cupboards
4. Drawers
5. Shelves

6. Closets
7. Hooks or racks
8. Baskets - all sizes
9. Boxes
10. Crates

♡ Everything needs its place. Decide what you need to get to store everything. (garage sales, stores, friends...keep looking) It's fun.

Leap Through the Laundry

1. Gather the dirty clothes and sort them.

Colored or dark clothes

White or light clothes

2. Check for stains and spots. (use a spray-on stain remover - check the clothing labels)

3. Check all pockets and remove many surprises.

4. Don't load washer too full. Use right amount of detergent (read the box)

5. Keep bleach away from colored or dark clothing.

6. Sometimes you may need to wash clothes every day. By doing this, it will help you not get behind.

As soon as clothes are dry, fold or hang up for less wrinkles.

*Hint - If you have heavy bedspreads, rugs... go to the laundromat to use larger machines.

While the clothes wash—keep moving...

Go attack the kitchen......➔

Attack the Kitchen

1. Pick up dirty dishes and pans and scrape off food.
   A. Check fridge, throw away yukky food, put dirty dishes in sink
2. Rinse or soak dishes in sink with hot sudsy water.
3. You have some choices
   A. Load dishwasher (if you have one)
   B. Wash, rinse, dry and put away dishes
   C. Soak dishes overnight (if you're too tired)
4. Clean off counters and stove top.
5. Sweep the floor and take out trash.
   A. Quickly wipe up spills and spots

♡ How long did this take? Run to the bathrooms.

Brighten the Bathrooms

1. Fold and hang up towels.
2. Tidy counters, replace toilet paper, (if empty) and empty trash.
3. Scour sink (tub too if needed) Have you tried the soap scum sprays?
4. Spray and clean mirror.

Breeze through the Bedrooms!

Label the drawers or use cut out pictures for children.

Socks   PJ's
Underwear

Shirts
Sweaters

Shorts   Pants

Hint: For small toys, cloth bags with a strong string can hold many things.

1. Make beds
2. Pick up clutter and clothes
3. Is there a place for everything?

It helps to tidy one room at a time.

GOOD JOB!

Sort children's clothes often. Find a place for "too small" clothes & shoes. Save better clothes for other children in the family and give the rest away (or save for a garage sale, etc.)

HOME SWEET HOME

1. Try to take an interest in your home.
2. Don't let housework get you down.
3. A tidy home makes everyone feel better.
4. Have a simple plan.
    A. Know what's for dinner.
    B. Know how to tidy clutter.
5. Learn to do basic cleaning.
6. Learn how the right colors make a pretty home.

Weekly Magic
Pick Your Day

Once a week things can be done to keep your home and personal things organized. The following are a few suggestions:

1. Clean and organize your purse and/or briefcase.
2. Clean toilets.
3. Vacuum and wash floors.
4. Laundry (if you're not doing it daily)
5. Main grocery shopping.
   Check those food sales and remember your coupons!
   (it helps to save coupons for foods & things you like)
6. Check closets, cupboards, and windows.
7. Wash the car and tidy inside. (organize glove compartment)

 Thank you for caring about your home.

2. MEALS
The Meal Hints

1. The kitchen is said to be the heart of the home. (try to learn to cook)

2. Do you know that to your family dinner is the most important meal of the day? (Think about it the night before or plan early - by 10 a.m.)

3. Prepare the healthful foods that are family favorites. (often)

4. Encourage helpers in the kitchen. (children love to help, invite Dad)

5. Try not to eat in front of the TV. (sometimes this is your only time together)

6. Talk about happy positive things during meal time.

7. Everyone gets to help clean up the dishes and put the food away.

1. Breakfast
2. Lunch
3. Dinner
4. Snacks...?

Always wash your hands with soap and water before preparing any food.

Meals and cooking do not have to be hard.

1. Decide what foods your family likes.

2. Learn how to plan your weekly menu and grocery shopping.

3. Look for food specials. Buy extras so your cupboards can offer "meals for busy days".

4. Learn how to cook smart.

Foods come in many ways.

1. Fresh
2. Frozen
3. Canned
4. Bottled
5. Boxed
6. Bagged

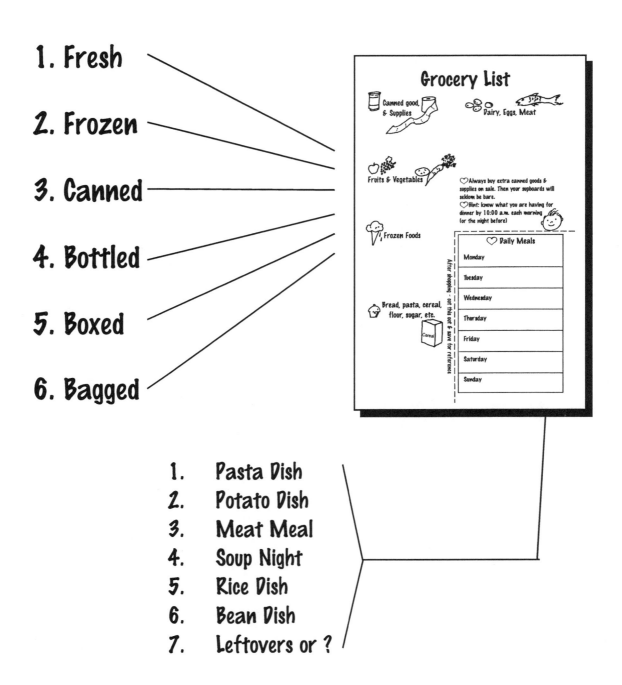

Grocery List

Canned good, & Supplies

Dairy, Eggs, Meat

Fruits & Vegetables

♡ Always buy extra canned goods & supplies on sale. Then your cupboards will seldom be bare.

♡ Hint: know what you are having for dinner by 10:00 a.m. each morning (or the night before)

Frozen Foods

After shopping - cut this out & save for reference

Bread, pasta, cereal, flour, sugar, etc.

Cereal

♡ Daily Meals

Monday	
Tuesday	
Wednesday	
Thursday	
Friday	
Saturday	
Sunday	

1. Pasta Dish
2. Potato Dish
3. Meat Meal
4. Soup Night
5. Rice Dish
6. Bean Dish
7. Leftovers or ?

Plan, prepare, and make it easy on yourself.

To Order Tablets See Chapter 9 — Mail Order Section

FRUIT

Try to eat more fruit and less candy and sugary things. Keep fresh fruit in the kitchen.

VEGETABLES

Try to serve fresh or frozen vegetables every night. Discover the vegetables your family enjoys the most.

These real foods are good for you and EASY to prepare.
(These are suggestions only. Many cultures have wonderful foods we have not listed. Please share your recipes with friends)

❀ Potatoes
❀ Rice
❀ Pasta
❀ Beans
❀ All vegetables
❀ All fruits

Always buy plenty of these foods. You don't need too much meat.
(which will help your grocery bill)

These other foods are needed in most recipes.

❀ Flour
❀ Sugar
❀ Spices, Flavorings
❀ Baking powder, Baking soda
❀ Salt and pepper
❀ Oil and shortening
❀ Eggs
❀ Milk
❀ Butter or Margarine
❀ Some meat

The more you cook the easier it gets.
(Keep your cupboards stocked)

Make sure your cupboards have wholesome foods.

Soups	Peanut Butter
Vegetables	Raisins
Fruit	Jam
Gelatin & Puddings	Crackers
Chocolate Drink Mix	Popcorn
Instant Potatoes	Powered Milk
Honey	Oatmeal

Keep these foods on hand all the time.
(don't waste money on soft drinks, chips, candy, cookies, sugary cereals - this is junk food)

POTATOES

You can make a meal out of potatoes. Be creative!

1. **Bake them:** Top with butter, salt & pepper, or grated cheese, or chili and cheese, or bacon bits and green onions and cheese.

2. **Steam them:** Red potatoes are delicious.

3. **Boil them:** (peel) Mash cooked potatoes with some milk. Serve with butter, dash of salt and pepper. Try different soup gravies on top. (mix 1 can beef stroganoff soup & 1 can cream chicken soup with 1 can milk.)

4. **Oven Baked Potatoes:** (don't peel) Cut up potatoes, toss with 2 Tablespoons oil, 1 envelope onion soup mix, chopped green onions, chopped green pepper, ¼ cup parmesan cheese. Bake 350° for 30-40 min.

* Always scrub potatoes before cooking.

 # BEANS

There are many varieties of beans. You can cook them yourself
(start the night before and follow directions on package)
or buy canned beans. (have your can opener ready!)

1. **Special Chili Beans:** Use 1 can chili, 1 can kidney beans, 1 can stewed tomatoes. Heat & serve. (add corn for a change)

2. **Bean Salad:** Drain the following beans: 1 can kidney, 1 can green beans, 1 can garbanzo, 1 can diced beets, ½ chopped red onion or dehydrated onion, 1 cup Italian dressing, ¼ cup sugar. Put in bowl, mix well, and refrigerate.

3. **White Bean Soup:** 2 cans of great northern white beans (don't drain). 1 slice of ham cut into small pieces. Simmer for 15 minutes. Try cornbread with this. (follow directions on box & use muffin liners)

4. **Pinto Beans and Rice:** Heat leftover rice and beans in separate pots or microwave. On each plate put 1 cup rice, pinto beans, chopped tomato, green onion, cucumber, grated cheese, sour cream, salsa.

5. **Super Soup:** 1 can stewed tomatoes, 1 can tomato soup, 1 can corn, 1 can kidney beans, 2 cups leftover pasta, leftover vegetables. Season to taste. Heat 5 minutes and serve.

RICE

Rice comes in many varieties.
White rice and brown rice are the most popular.
(when you're too busy, minute rice works great)
Cook rice
(follow package directions carefully and double recipe for extra rice dishes)

1. Hot rice: Serve with butter & salt, gravy or sauces. (use instead of potato)

2. Casseroles: Chicken, tuna, ground beef —check your cookbooks and magazines.

3. Stir fry (use leftover rice): Put steamed vegetables over rice with a dash of soy sauce.

4. Speedy spanish rice: Put ¼ cup salsa into your rice cooking water. Add rice and cook. Serve with a little grated cheese.

5. Rapid rice pudding: Cook one package (large 5 oz.) vanilla pudding. Fold in two cups of plain leftover rice, stir in 1 teaspoon cinnamon. (add raisins for variety)

6. Soups: Add leftover rice to most soups for extra nutrition.

PASTA

1. **Pasta comes in all sizes and shapes and colors.**

   (spaghetti is only one of many pastas)

2. **When you're shopping look at all the different pastas. Try some of the following ideas.**

Serve a green salad or vegetables with all these meals.

Spaghetti — Try canned sauce when you're too busy to make homemade. Add some chopped tomatoes. Try new sauces too.

Lasagna — Easy when you use canned sauce. Follow directions on box. (Freezes well)

Pasta Noodles (try shells, macaroni, etc.) — Good with sauces, in vegetable salads, or butter and a little seasoned salt. Serve with steamed veggies.

Macaroni and Cheese (once in a while) — You can make homemade or buy the boxes. Try cooked hot dog slices or other meat pieces.

Flat Noodles — Try a tuna or chicken casserole: Mix cooked noodles with 1 can cream of mushroom soup, 1 soup can of milk. Layer cooked noodles, drained tuna, grated cheese, noodles, more grated cheese, and crushed potato chips on top. Bake at 350° for 30 min.

♡ Have fun experimenting!

3. Treasures

Sometimes a few
good hints can make
a big difference!

Grandma's Treasured Hints

1. If you work too much - learn to play.
   If you play too much - learn to work.

2. Find a reason to laugh every day.

3. Never let the gas in your car get below ¼ tank.

4. Have a bubble bath.

5. You know you're growing up when you don't blame others.

6. Find an exercise you like - it becomes fun.

7. Feeling sorry for yourself only makes things worse.

8. Make yourself do something nice for someone else.

9. A good night's sleep makes a better day.

10. Keep a money jar to use for something special.

11. Always show appreciation when you receive a gift or kindness.

12. Wash your face, comb your hair, and shave before breakfast.

13. If you look washed out, grab some lipstick and blush.

14. When the family comes home, get off the phone.

15. Practice being a kind person.

16. Avoid debt like the plague - pay off those bills.

17.   Remember you're in charge of your happiness.

18.   Be loyal to your family.   Be a true friend.

19.   If you spend too much, <u>stop spending</u> and learn to save. If you are the opposite and won't spend, lighten up and help out more.

20.   Give to others because you want to, not because you expect something in return.

21.   Take Care of Yourself: Bathe or shower daily; brush & floss daily; comb & brush hair daily.

22.   There's an old saying: "When you're having a bad day, clean out your sock drawer." (Clean out anything!)

23.   Take a few minutes and plant a garden.

24.   Don't loan anything if it means too much to you.

25.   Develop a grateful heart for all the things you already have.

26.   Remember to say the good things about your Mother and/or Father. Don't dig up the worn past; it is time to move forward.

27.   Take a 10 minute break and do something you like.

28.   If you borrow, always return it promptly.

29.   When you're wrong, admit it and don't do it again.

30.   Everyone looks forward to dinner by at least 6 p.m.

31.   …and finally, if you feel you are now an adult, it is time to let go of childish ways: Whenever you leave the house, dress decent (no sloppy clothes, don't show too much skin, & get a nice haircut) and be clean and respectable.

Children deserve caring parents who try to be good examples

♡ **Hints can only be "helpful" if you try to do what they say…**

Thank you
for
Loving
Children

IX
Mail Order and Special Helps
Helpful and Thoughtful Products and Ideas that make life
easier for parents of young children.

WHAT IS A LEARNING PROBLEM?

Did you know that everyone has some kind of a learning problem?
Some Teachers understand these difficulties more than others.
If you had any of the following problems, one or more of your children may have them too.

- Did you ever have problems in school because you couldn't concentrate or focus?

- Were certain things difficult, like reading and/or math?

- Did you have a difficult time being organized and understanding all of the assignments the teacher gave you?

- Did you dislike homework, and even if you got it done, you forgot to turn it in?

- Were you bored and/or confused or unable to sit still?

- Did going to school make you feel stressful and unhappy?

- Did you feel like no one understood you?

The above comments are a few of the learning difficulties people experience. Some of the names that are given to these learning blocks are dyslexia, ADD (Attention Deficit Disorder), ADHD (Attention Deficit Hyperactivity Disorder), etc.

Call CAREMORE for more information in regard to hands-on education/training and assistance to help families learn how to remove learning blocks. Finally there are real answers and help (without the use of drugs like Ritilin)!
(435) 634-9510

MAKE YOUR OWN CHARTS & TABLETS
Entire 25 Template Set - Only $7.95

8½" x 11" charts

Loving Children Chart

Birthday Chart

Hugs Chart

BDB Chart

Love/Safe Chart

Time Out Room

God & Goodness Chart

Children's ID Cards

Inexpensive Play Recipes
Fun Stuff for Kids
(Pamphlet)

Home Sweet Home Chart

House Hints Chart

Book Marks

MAKE YOUR OWN CHARTS & TABLETS

Tablets (5½" x 8 ")

Easy Letter Tablet

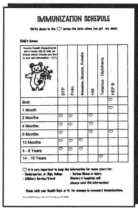

Immunization Tablet

Thank-you NotesTablet

Babysitter Helper Tablet

Doctor Helper Record

Grocery & Menu Helper

Small Tablets (5½" x 4 ")

Where to Find Me

Telephone Messages

Important Numbers

Large Tablets (8½" x 11 ")

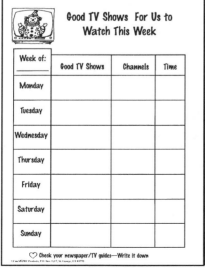

Good TV Shows

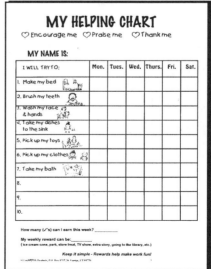

Fun Helping Chart

Color Mee Cards

Crayons included FREE!

LARGE 5½" X 8½"

When do you want to go for a treat? Date you can go:____

From:____

To My BEST Friend!!

Love:____

Because of you, everything seems better...
Thank you Thank you Thank you

Love:____

Get Well Very, Very, very, very SOON! (Sorry you aren't feeling bouncy)

Love:____

We can wish YOU a Happy, Happy Birthday!

From:____

I can wish you a very HAPPY BIRTHDAY

Love:____

I LOVE YOU! (Thank you for all you do)...

Love:____

So we can play and do something FUN!...

Love:____

Dear Mommy Dear Daddy

by Marie Foss Hafen

CareMORE Products
P.O. Box 4217
St. George, UT 84770
1-435-634-9510

Dear Friends, We are thrilled with the positive responses we are receiving about the book. Would you be so kind to send us successful comments and stories as to how the book, Dear Mommy Dear Daddy, has helped you, your family, friends or organization. (For your participation we will send you a FREE ☐ *"Holiday Ideas for Children"* OR ☐ *"Home Parties for Kids & Play Stuff Recipes" (leaflet)*, OR *one of the charts on page 145*. Choose one. _____(Your success may be the turning point in helping others.) Carefully remove this page, write your comments below and mail to the above address. We look forward to hearing from you!!
Warm Wishes, Marie & Staff

- -

Name:_____ Phone Number: _____

Address: _____

_____

Please write the ages of your children _____

Age of Mom_____ Age of Dad_____

Comments: (Look through the book and write down the things that helped you the most?)

_____

_____

_____

_____

_____

_____

_____

_____

_____

_____

_____

_____

"You can make a difference!"
BY DONATING BOOKS
Help your community by helping new moms.

Many families need basic parenting educational help. Parenting and unwed mother
classes, struggling young parents, hospitals, family advocate organizations and
special family task groups are anxiously requesting this simple to read (and understand),
illustrated parenting book, written as if by the baby and young child.
THANK YOU FOR CARING ABOUT FAMILIES!

EACH BOOK REPRESENTS GIVING HELP TO ONE FAMILY OR 3-10 PEOPLE:

❑ **English** version
❑ **Spanish** version

❑ 2 Books = $29.50
❑ 5 Books = $74.00
❑ 10 Books = $149.00
❑ 15 Books = $224.00

❑ 20 Books = $299.00
❑ 1 Case (36 books) = $538.00
❑ 2 Cases (72 books) = $1,075.00
❑ (   ) Cases _____ = $_____
($14.95 per book)

(Your) Name:_____ (or) Company or Organization Name: _____

Address: _____

Phone Number: _____ Fax Number: _____

Number of books you are ordering:_____Paid by: Approved check or Money Order _____

Master Card or Visa (number):_____Expires: _____

For credit card orders call 435-634-0853

Signature: _____

(Purchase Order Number):_____Approved by: _____

Books are being donated to:

✔ *Hospital Prenatal & New Mom Classes*   ✔ *Abuse Shelters / Homes*

✔ *Parenting & Unwed Mother Education*

✔ *Community outreach Programs; Family Advocate organizations: (United Way, Headstart, Health Depts./WIC,*
County & State Agencies, Detention Centers, Rehabs. Police Dept. programs, etc.)

Name of Organization you are donating to: _____

Shipping Address: _____

_____

Phone: _____ Contact person (Director, etc.) _____

Please write your name as you would like it to appear in the book: _____

Label Sample for each book: This book has been donated by _____ because we care about families.

Please mail this order page and your check or money order to:
CareMore Products Inc.
P.O. Box 4217, St. George, UT 84770
435-634-0853   Fax 435-634-9510

When placing order, cut order sheet out or make copies of this form.

QTY.	PRODUCT	PRICE	TOTAL
	PARENTING BOOK		
	Parenting Book (Dear Mommy Dear Daddy) English	$ 14.95	
	Parenting Book (Dear Mommy Dear Daddy) Spanish	$ 14.95	
	MAKE YOUR OWN CHARTS & TABLETS	$ 7.95	
	COLOR MEE (Black & White) GREETING CARDS		
	Pkg of 10 greeting cards/envelopes & FREE crayons		
	5½" x 8½" (only $1.10 per card)	$ 10.95	
	ORGANIZATIONS		
	Non Profit Organizations can request a form showing Volume Book Discounts		

MAIL TO: CareMORE Products
P.O. Box 4217
St. George, UT 84770
**FOR VISA or MASTER CARD
ORDERS CALL:**
1-435-634-0853 or FAX 1-435-634-9510

SHIPPING CHART

For orders totalling	Add
$ .99 - $20.00	$4.00
$21.00 - 40.00	$6.00
$41.00 - 75.00	$9.00
over $75.00	$12.00

SUBTOTAL

Utah residents add
6.25% sales tax

SHIPPING

TOTAL

Prices subject to change without notice

Name _____

Phone _____ Address _____

City_____ State_____ Zip _____

Charge Card # _____

Card: ☐ Master Card   ☐ Visa   Expiration Date_____

Signature_____

CareMORE Products
P.O. Box 4217
St. George, UT 84770